ADVANCE PRAISE

"Whether or not you are in the public eye, keeping yourself protected online is more important now than ever. This book is a must-read to protect your business, yourself, and your family."

—JUSTIN GUARINI, *American Idol*

"If you want to stay on top, you have to keep climbing. *UnHACKD* gives you all the tools to scale the cyber security mountain peak."

—DENNIS YU, BlitzMetrics

"If you ever plan on 'Googling' something or merely turning on a computer again, this book is a must. Humorous and easy to read, *UnHACKD* is filled with practical advice to protect your data, reputation, and family online."

—KIM WALSH-PHILLIPS, Powerful Professionals

"This book is for you, me, my children, and the author's aunt. Seriously, it is for everyone. *UnHACKD* gives practical advice on how to protect our identity, our money, and our privacy with technology. All that with real-world examples and a sense of humor!"

—MARNIE STOCKMAN, Lifecycle Insights

UNHACKD

CYBER SECURITY ESSENTIALS TO PROTECT YOUR BUSINESS AND YOUR IDENTITY

...a cyber "health" insurance for your business and family!

HOWARD GLOBUS

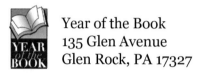

Year of the Book
135 Glen Avenue
Glen Rock, PA 17327

Print ISBN: 978-1-64649-110-0
Ebook ISBN: 978-1-64649-111-7

CONTENTS

Introduction 1

1 | Go Google Yourself 7

2 | Financial Awareness................................... 21

3 | Phishing for Gold.. 37

4 | Beware of Social Triggers........................ 45

5 | Out-of-the-Box Vulnerabilities 65

6 | A Matter of Trust..................................... 79

7 | Password Management 89

8 | Backups... 95

9 | Future Threats & The Internet of Things 107

Conclusion 115

INTRODUCTION

Why write another book on cybersecurity?

I guess the real question is: "Has anybody actually read a book on cybersecurity?" There are many out there that share the specifics of notorious cybersecurity attacks, but are there really any books that teach you how to keep yourself safe and avoid being hacked in the future?

You may have stumbled across an article online or wandered into a TED talk touting the "3 Steps to Protect Yourself Online," but there is not yet a comprehensive guide to help individuals and business owners successfully navigate the shark-infested waters of cyber-security.

The goal of this current volume is to bring you examples of the kinds of questions I've been asked about by a wide variety of people—from family like my mother-in-law, cousins, and an elderly uncle who was thinking about buying cryptocurrency, to business customers actively searching for a method to keep themselves and their organizations safe.

Who should read this book on cybersecurity? Obviously, as the author, I would hope everyone would read this book. Hubris aside, I think small business owners, managers, chief operating officers, laypeople, and parents have the most to benefit. So much of our daily lives are spent online, from banking and business to socialization and education, no one can really afford to rely on the tired trope "I'm just not that good at computers." You don't need to be an expert car mechanic to drive safely and avoid disastrous accidents. My argument is that we should know the rules of the road and the pitfalls and potential dangers while we live our lives online. The dangers are real, and they cannot be avoided by not educating ourselves.

A good defense is not, and cannot be "Because I don't know how to do it, it probably can't be done." Instead let's bring the complex to a comprehensible discussion in plain English.

To get oriented in today's interconnected world, we'll start our journey together with some things I think everyone should know—like searching for yourself online and discovering what information is exposed. That way you have a better idea about what steps you need to take for your safety.

We will also focus on financial awareness, including key differences between business and personal accounts, and what possibilities exist for account compromise. And of course, what you can do to prevent that from happening!

This is especially relevant today, as the IRS and U.S. government prepare to roll out $300-per-month per-child tax credit payments. As often occurs when new financial assistance programs are launched and go into effect, the scammers come out. In this instance there are already reports of scammers contacting families offering to expedite their payments, get them a yearly lump sum payment per child, or "informing" that overpayments have been made and the IRS is demanding repayment over the phone. Being armed with basic knowledge—such as the fact that the IRS or federal government will never contact you by phone and demand payment immediately—can help you not only through this series of scams but future cons as well.

Being armed with basic knowledge will help you not only avoid current scams, but future cons as well.

Next you'll learn about phishing—a targeted attack by email spam, instant messages or the like—where a piece or two of publicly available information about you is used to create a sense of familiarity, so that you will take an action that is not in your best interest.

We'll discuss Social Triggers—how societal norms and preconditioning set us up to make certain automatic responses—and how those unconscious responses can be used maliciously as a threat.

Once you know how to keep an eye out for them, you'll be better prepared to keep yourself safe.

During COVID there was an increase in targeted phishing attacks where large money transfers were requested of CFOs or operations managers responsible for money transfers. These attackers took advantage of people not being in the same physical space while many worked from home, making double confirmations more difficult. Using techniques where business emails are compromised and official-looking requests are made, many companies fell victim to tricks that rely on email, loosely documented processes, and social triggers to obtain compliance and action.

Another vulnerability we'll delve into is the problem with default passwords for the electronics within your home that can be used to gain access to your personal network, thereby creating opportunities for mischief, as well as how to protect yourself from cyberattack that might result from someone impersonating a trusted delivery person or repairman.

We'll continue the conversation with password management and why it is so key to protecting everything you hold dear. Password complexity is important to keeping your accounts secure, but the more complex you make a password, the less likely you are to remember it. We'll examine different password management tools to help you streamline this process in both business and family environments.

Year after year, studies show that weak passwords are prevalent in personal and business transactions alike. The easiest way to compromise a system is to use easy to guess or crack passwords. Many of the attacks that make the news bootstrap off of a simple incursion that is the result of one weak password. An example is a weak password for a golf course's wi-fi in the clubhouse and meeting rooms, where vulnerable, unpatched machines may connect to one or two hundred business people attending a fundraising event. The sponsors and business people who connect a device to the wi-fi make themselves vulnerable. An attack on hundreds or thousands of companies can emanate from one such poorly managed password at a public space.

We'll also talk about backups—a catch phrase for all manner of data storage and duplication for safekeeping—and help you discern what you need to back up, how often, and how to prioritize your efforts so you will be able to quickly restore all your data in the event of loss.

Finally we move on to the "Internet of Things"—the concept of connecting every device in your home to the internet, so you might turn up the thermostat when you're on your way home in winter, or switch on the lights while you're away on vacation, or monitor your children and their nanny throughout the workday. There are pros and cons to all these opportunities, and this chapter will help guide you through the exercise of thinking through the convenience versus the security questions.

Benjamin Franklin said, "Those who would give up essential liberty to purchase a little temporary safety, deserve neither liberty nor safety." This quote is often used in security discussions and "liberty" is often replaced with "privacy" to make a point related to the sanctity of privacy.

The quote actually relates to a question of taxes versus defense spending, but that's not why I write about it here. The point I want to make is that in all facets of life we have to make choices. These decisions then build on past choices and so forth. The sequence of decisions sets us down one road and sometimes closes off other options.

Convenience over privacy, cheap over secure, easy-to-understand over thought-provoking...

Each decision has consequences.

What does that have to do with cybersecurity? When we choose convenience over privacy, cheap over secure, easy-to-understand over thought-provoking, we make choices... choices that have consequences. The consequences, both individually and as a society or purchasing class, may not manifest in the near term. However, in the larger picture, choices dictate future outcomes, years down the road.

Given the gravity of the consequences, can any of us afford to blithely use technology or tools and claim we don't really need to know too much about them? As stewards of our futures we owe it to ourselves and our children and grandchildren to make an attempt to understand the consequences of our choices today and how we use our tools.

Or we can all go back to playing "Candy Crush" and let someone more knowledgeable make those choices for us. I am sure they have our best interests at heart.

CHAPTER 1

GO GOOGLE YOURSELF

As a parent of two young teenagers, I routinely had long conversations about all things internet. I tried to explain to my children that everything they posted to social media and the web would be out there, forever. They countered by trying to school me that posts like Instagram Live stories are removed after 24 hours, and that SnapChat group chats are deleted after a similar amount of time. They even touted that simple "Snaps" evaporate after *just 10 seconds.*

"But what happens when one member of the group takes a screenshot of the chat and reposts it to their Facebook feed?" I hinted. "Never mind when the platform itself has a data breach." Their blank stares suggested their only frame of reference for the words "data breach" came from television shows involving international espionage on a massive scale.

"Not only would your content be at risk, but also your credit card data." Of course at that point, it was my credit card data on the line, so small wonder they felt no obvious concern.

"Even your UserID and password can be transferred to less than reliable hands. Would you want your sibling to be able to log into your SnapChat account and post as if it were you?"

Flash forward years later for my teens, and now they are beginning to understand that all their data was being stored from the moment they posted to their favorite hashtag of the week. It was also hacked when the service that housed that content was breached. Proving my point.

You need to understand that what you're creating *now* is a record that will exist and follow you around throughout life and beyond.

Can you hear me now?

The slightly older crowd will have grown up hearing the phrase "This will go down on your permanent record" uttered by school administrators. While this myth is a terrific line for a Violent Femmes song, most of us discovered no one at college or our first jobs cared a whit about what went down in middle school. Those so-called permanent records went the way of vinyl. But just like vinyl records, the interactions we have on social media will likely have a resurgence at some point... and when they do, they'll leave permanent footprints.

Content you create is not only searchable... it's findable.

In some countries there are measures which can be taken to request that online data and personal accounts be destroyed. There are statutes such as the "Right to Be Forgotten" law, also known as the "Right to Erasure." It is a rule granting citizens of the European Union the right and the power to demand that data about them be deleted. Since 2014, EU citizens have had the right to request that links to any sensitive personal information about them be removed as well.

Then in 2016, the General Data Protection Regulation (GDRP) was passed—again regulating action within the European Union regarding data protection—safeguarding their citizens' privacy rights and this time including measures for financial penalties and restitution.

However, for U.S. citizens these types of laws do not exist. Quite frankly there is even question about where data in the EU is being stored, and whether the Right to Be Forgotten law was even being practiced properly in the first place.

The point for young and old is that we need to acknowledge that our data—along with the content we create—is not only searchable... but findable. It is freely available. Go Google yourself. Up comes direct links to all your media accounts, websites, videos, and life's most embarrassing moments. You may be surprised and horrified to discover pictures of yourself from fifteen years ago, which prompt you to wish you were now as overweight as you thought you were back then.

Perhaps you may not personally find the dirtiest of your dirt on a simple web search, but if an employer is researching your background, you can be darned sure they will have access to your embarrassing middle name, every address at which you've ever resided, your true biological age, past and present marital status, complete work history, education, driving record, criminal record, drug screening results, medical history, and all the damning pictorial evidence shared by your social media BFFs.

If you're applying for the military or any position that needs clearances, then the FBI will additionally learn every whirl and swirl of you, right down to those fingerprints taken for your fourth-grade Science Fair experiment.

And if you have political aspirations? Well, you should probably consider everything you ever wrote in someone else's high school yearbook, and any video that shows you dancing. Everything is fodder for the universe.

In ages past, deep searches were doable but difficult. Now however, they are well within the realm of mere mortals. Everything from the crazy drinking parties of your youth, to pictures of you smoking or participating in drug activity, to sexting pictures to a boyfriend or girlfriend.

Imagine two seventeen-year-olds texting less than innocent pictures to one another. Never mind that they may be in a relationship at the time, or even that the sexting may have been consensual... when this activity is undertaken by underage children, both the sender and the receiver become in breach of child pornography laws, because they are in possession of images of a sexual nature of an underage individual.

You need to be very careful and curate what you post to the web or transmit via electronic means. This is important for young people, but also for parents and grandparents... not only for yourself, but for sharing with loved ones.

Okay, boomer

Once social media applications and websites became ubiquitous in the early 2000s, parents started documenting their children's lives, from conception to adulthood. These photos may not only later prove embarrassing, but in some cases they can be compromising or destroy anonymity.

The family photos we once carried around with us in our wallets or purses have been replaced. We no longer have just the most recent standard-issue, assembly-line school photo, but also everything from sonograms, birthdays, and graduations... to last night's poor table manners. The concept of privacy is all but dead, because these photos are viewable and instantly sharable.

The retort I get from my children is, "I have nothing to hide," which may in fact be true at age 13 or 15 or 22. Later in life those same photos, texts, emails, or blog posts may be perceived in a much different way. What was innocuous at an earlier age may ten years later get you banned from ever hosting the Oscars, like Kevin Hart's terror tweets that his son might turn out to be gay, and his subsequent declaration of intention to prevent that in any way possible. Many celebrity personalities have lived to regret an off-hand remark or past stand that has not aged any better than Keith Richards.

The Governor of Virginia, Ralph Northam, was nearly dismissed from his position after a photograph of him appearing in blackface *35 years earlier* in a medical school yearbook that was distributed to the press. Gov. Northam later admitted to being one of the men in the photo and promised to "do better," but then the following day recanted his acknowledgment and denied being either of the men pictured (one in blackface, the other in Ku Klux Klan robes). This took over the media cycle and prompted Eastern Virginia Medical School to launch an inquiry that lasted four months, ultimately reporting its inability to determine the identity of either man in the photograph.

Today's "off-hand" remarks may be far less innocuous in decades to come.

Similarly, Canadian Prime Minister Justin Trudeau was called out publicly when *Time* magazine printed a photograph of him in brownface, dressed as an Arabian prince, from a 2001 party at a private school where he was teaching that term. He later confessed to having also worn blackface when appearing in a high school performance of the Jamaican song "Day-O" written by the African-American singer and civil rights activist Harry Belafonte. Would Trudeau's high school costume have been racially noteworthy in the year the production was performed? Maybe not. But now it raises far more than an eyebrow, considering the politics of the day and that at the time of the scandal he was Prime Minister of Canada and not a teacher or student.

Will these "scandals" become less important over time? Maybe, maybe not.

When Supreme Court Justice Brett Kavanaugh was being vetted for his lifetime appointment, he was embroiled in controversy related to college behavior of alleged sexual assault and drunken debauchery with underage students in the same house. Documents, notes, and emails surfaced that included a letter from Kavanaugh to friends that detailed how crazy they were going to be over the summer in a house they had rented, stating they might want to warn the neighbors.

A hundred years ago this would've been dismissed as "boys being boys" but these days it is certainly seen in a different light—more of a spotlight under high beams—where it will be analyzed and scrutinized. What was acceptable 20 years ago is no longer business as usual.

Consider actions attributed to Harvey Weinstein that were wretched and boorish yet commonplace in the entertainment industry for decades past, but which have now landed him in jail for possibly the rest of his life. These same actions—currently classified as *rape* and *predatory sexual assault*—are things he would've gotten away with 50 years beforehand.

I'm not condoning such behavior by any means, but we need to consider and re-consider how our actions today may be construed differently in the future.

Think of other perennial "heroes" who have been re-judged based on the social mores of today. Columbus Day was first celebrated in San Francisco in 1869, as a commemoration of Christopher Columbus's achievements as well as a celebration of Italian-American heritage, then later became a federal holiday in 1937. While Columbus the explorer may have been contentious in the 1970s when alternative holidays like "Indigenous People's Day" were proposed, today he's downright vilified in connection with the beginnings of the transatlantic slave trade and the deaths of millions of indigenous people from smallpox and influenza.

The ultimate point of sharing these examples of public figures who've been later embarrassed by the documentation of their actions is this. For any data you share—now, in the past, and in the future—you will have no control of it once released.

Likewise, we should be cognizant of the word choices we make in addition to the pictures we take. When speaking with my kids, I mention legal cases I've been involved with. In one, a broker had spoken derogatorily about his clients. When emails were read out in court, attorneys shared excerpts such as the broker calling his client a "melonhead who didn't know shit." What might have been a harmless email between colleagues became a public embarrassment, even though the bulk of his correspondence was of a more professional tone.

A good rule to remember is: Don't write or send anything you wouldn't want your mother or grandmother to read in the papers. Do not put anything into writing or post to the internet that which you would not want to have read out in a court of law, or documented in the *New York Times*, even taken out of context.

As an aside, the plaintiff in the "melonhead" case actually received a multimillion-dollar settlement because he had been misled by his broker, not to mention the millions it cost to defend that lawsuit.

What Google knows

You should also take into consideration what friends and relatives will find when they Google you.

For one man featured in an NPR story, the repercussions were dynamic when his future in-laws uncovered a charge of *statutory rape* on a criminal record discovered through a Google search. The charge had been written up in a local newspaper at the time, and although he had been 17 and his girlfriend was 16—and even though it was consensual on her part—the girlfriend's parents had pressed charges. Not only was it very hard for this man's future in-laws to get past this, but it was also difficult for his fiancée.

Such information is available to future schools or college officials. If you weren't already aware, you should understand that most upper-level entrance administrators automatically perform internet searches regarding individuals applying to their program. While most surface-level background checks won't include a search of court records, in highly competitive or compensated fields—or fields in which the individual would have a media presence—a much deeper background check will be done.

You have no control over your data once you post it.

If you've ever been tempted to lie about your qualifications, consider the fate of politicians, talk show hosts, and news anchors who faked their backgrounds. Former NBC news anchor Brian Williams was taken down in 2015 for claiming to be somewhere in a war zone when he was not. Disgraced and suspended for six months, he had to reinvent his career as an eleventh-hour news anchor for MSNBC. While he's certainly not destitute, this embarrassing issue has become a top-ranked result when searching his name.

In short, your social media posts and online interactions can have serious and lasting consequences. Nothing is private. And not all jokes are actually funny. Now, or in the future.

The dark web

In the early 2010s, there was a popular website that served as an aggregation point for semi-organized thieves. People with malicious intent could subscribe to this service on the dark web which would cull through ZIP codes or residential blocks to find when people were going on vacation based on content posted to their social media.

These thieves would then orchestrate their burglaries in a methodical manner, rather than hitting one house and then taking a week off to plan their next robbery. They could often steal from multiple homes in a single neighborhood in a single night, knowing the chance of being found out or discovered by someone coming home was low.

The firm Credit Sesame interviewed 50 ex-burglars in England and discovered a shocking 80% had used data culled from Facebook, Twitter, Google Street View, and Foursquare to plan robberies.

When people post pictures from home, they rarely consider what's in the background of the photos. Or even more dangerously, perhaps they want to highlight the setting—expensive artwork, grandma's silver, or a new big-screen TV. When this data is later correlated by a thief after someone announces they will be on vacation, it not only lets the potential burglar know you won't be home, but allows them to make a "shopping list" of most desirable items.

80% of surveyed burglars culled social media data to plan robberies.

Another thing to consider about your posting habits is whether you may inadvertently assist a thief to stake out your home based on your travel patterns. For example, if you tweet out things like: "I hate to go to work at 8am everyday" or "This is the second time I've had to stay till 9 o'clock at night" or "It's the third weekend in a row when I've had to work all day Saturday and Sunday," you are essentially dictating the perfect targeting times for theft.

There are a number of cases in recent history of criminals tracking the comings and goings of children based on photos and texts, shared either by the child, parent, or caregiver, commenting about when they are home or if children will be coming home to an empty house. Other seemingly innocent shared details might include the names of schools the children attend, what buses they ride, or if they walk home, as well as posting of practice times, lesson times, and game schedules.

Photographs that include a vehicle can allow criminals to know the make, model, and color of your family car, as well as possibly the license plate number. Think about how this information could be used (worst-case) for nefarious purposes. Also consider whether your photos are GEO-tagged. A criminal could potentially pinpoint the precise location of your child or loved one, day or night—a feat most parents would envy.

Photos of yourself and children, used for other purposes

The use of stock photos for promotional materials or website photos has waned over recent years, in large part because people see these same stock photos across multiple sites and soon disconnect, no longer resonating with what the company or product has to offer. It just feels too cookie-cutter.

In response, a number of groups have begun harvesting photos from social media platforms and repurposing them for their own uses through Photoshop or collage projects. This may appear innocuous on the surface, especially when it's someone else's photos. But what if you wake up tomorrow to find one or more of your family images is being used in a religious or political ad campaign? What if your photo has been repurposed on the website of a particular organization which goes against every one of your personal core values? This will no doubt be disconcerting... but the truth is, there's very little recourse for you to demand a website to take those pictures down.

Take this dilemma one step further and you'll discover there's a kink for everyone out there. Perhaps you were super thrilled with your recent footwear purchase, but feel infinitely less proud when the image of your tootsies later appears on ShoeFetishClub.com.

Even your selfies with weight loss goals could be shared in a salacious manner. Just because you only posted it to a "private" accountability group does not mean that content cannot be reposted or duplicated using screen-capture, later to be exploited by a rival or jealous adversary.

You don't have to date a celebrity to be burned by revenge porn like Blac Chyna, whose nude photos were posted to Instagram once her relationship with Robert Kardashian, Jr., turned sour. Just imagine the shock and horror one day when their child Dream scrolls back through Dad's Insta-feed to see pictures of herself wearing a cute watermelon outfit at the beach, only to discover Mom's melons exhibited for the world instead.

This kind of embarrassment isn't limited to internet scandals. It can be as simple as passing around your phone at a party to show off innocent pictures... meanwhile curious friends and family scroll further than you intended and discover what you were really up to on your last vacation.

Even if you keep a tight rein on the videos you store on your phone, remember that your content—or that of your partner or spouse—may be backed up to a cloud service or synched to data storage at a place of business.

Taken to a disturbing conclusion, even the pictures or videos snapped of your infant in the bathtub, or your toddler who likes to run naked through sprinklers in the summer, are cute and harmless as long as no one uses them in inappropriate ways. However, more important is to consider the legal ramifications of someone possessing such pictures in an era when pedophilia charges run rampant. Is this content you would like to have available to a potential college admin, or counselor, or your boss or a political rival?

The level of vitriol created when a video of Alexandria Ocasio-Cortez doing an imitation of the dance scene from *Breakfast Club* surfaced on Twitter—even in a video where no one was naked, or doing anything but the dance—was astonishing. While Rep. Ocasio-Cortez was being sworn in as a congresswoman in January 2019, social media was busy reviewing her imitation of Ally Sheedy's dance moves. Hours of time were wasted on both right- and left-wing sides of the media, either attacking or defending this completely innocuous recording from her youth. Imagine if there had been something more potentially damaging in this video.

Cyber-bullying

Cyber-bullying is real. It's also possible that an individual can find themselves on both sides of the cyber-bullying coin. There's a growing movement to allow zero tolerance of bullying in schools, including what gets posted online by students, both in and outside of the classroom.

Parents rarely want to believe their child would bully or intimidate someone else, but by seeing what your child posts on social media viewed through an impartial lens, some of those comments, statements, or acts may be seen as cyber-bullying.

This act is not limited to school-age children, however. It affects grown-ups too. "Hostile work environments" are often cited when personal social media is entered into evidence when those posts have been directed at an individual. That bleeds over into other areas of life. The question becomes: How do you protect against cyber bullying, but also allow for free speech?

An example would be someone speaking badly about a prior friend to a current friend, and sharing an embarrassing or awkward moment. What happens when the current friend either posts this "secret" or shares it publicly some other way, then later has a falling out? Even when former friends mention this inappropriate share, could it potentially be seen as cyber-bullying?

By the same token, groups do gang up on an individual and make them feel so badly about themselves that they have attempted or committed suicide. Other people have been teased online to the point of bringing weapons to school or work and either attempting—or succeeding—in hurting or killing one or more people, often including themselves.

How far is too far when protecting yourself and your loved ones?

How far is too far when attempting to protect yourself and loved ones from bullying?

Taken to extremes

In some cases, there's a potential for bribery or blackmail. When you're in a private online group, or a group chat or text, and anywhere information is shared that may not put you in a good light—or may compromise you in some other way—you open yourself to future bribery or blackmail.

A gay high school quarterback posted to a number of social chat applications and Instagram groups. His father was the CFO of a company and its business competitor was looking to gain an advantage. During deep opposition research, the rival company discovered the coming-out stories of this still-closeted high school quarterback.

The rival business had someone subversively entice the young man into a relationship where additional information and photographs were exchanged. Then the quarterback was approached by an agent of the rival company and threatened with being "outed" to his conservative religious parents.

But he was offered a way out, one that didn't involve him being outed! The quarterback could protect himself by inserting a USB drive—provided by his anonymous contact—into his father's work laptop. As CFO, the father was privy to financial information, forecasting, bank records, and personal data from members of the board, and had access to numerous documents related to the health of the company.

The young man ended up confessing to his father, feeling that the betrayal of trust was worse than any pain that might result from being exposed as gay. But not before the damage was done. Malware rolled through the entire corporation. Proprietary information was lost, and it was embarrassing all the way around.

Data lives forever on the internet

Email passes through many servers to get from a sender to the recipient, and very often copies are stored on each virtual hop. Likewise, once you release a photo, an email, text, or video to someone else, you rarely ever have control over where it will go next.

Almost all data is retrievable... for a fee.

Unless the device or machine is degaussed with a magnet, or its hard drives are destroyed with a drill or a crusher, data is almost always retrievable. The question becomes: How much are you willing to spend to retrieve it?

In my business designing and installing computer networks, software, and security, when I explain to clients that they can retrieve data "lost" from their laptops—including precious family photos, bank records, and bank statements—but that it may cost several thousands of dollars to do so, very often these clients prefer not to pursue it, instead losing all their personal data and content.

However, when the federal government wants data from a laptop, or a competitor wants access to trade secrets, or a foreign government is looking to blackmail a political candidate or steal intellectual property, that entity may be perfectly willing to spend tens of thousands—or even hundreds of thousands—to retrieve such data.

As we ponder the sky-high costs associated with data retrieval, we should also consider the importance of financial awareness in general, in an age in which our children may believe the ATM machine magically prints money on demand. But just as our parents warned us, money doesn't grow on trees, nor does it 3D print from a plastic debit card.

CHAPTER 2

FINANCIAL AWARENESS FOR YOU, YOUR KIDS, AND YOUR PARENTS

I had a friend who was a typical college kid. In the process of sprouting his wings of independence, he ran up huge credit card debt. That independence came back to bite him when he eventually discovered he had to pay the money back... all by himself. This caused an enormous amount of financial stress in his post-college life. Dealing with student loan debt is usually enough of a crisis, but adding significant credit card debt to the mix is like pouring kerosene over a bonfire.

Cash vs. Credit – Purchase protection limits

To dig himself out of debt, my friend employed a cash-only technique. Everything he wanted to purchase in the future had to be paid for in cash. If my friend didn't have the cash, then he couldn't buy it. Sounds smart, right? Here's where it can go wrong.

He eventually married, and on a shopping trip, he and his wife found a couch they wanted to purchase. My friend still didn't have a lot of money, but they'd saved especially for this special piece of furniture. The store was offering a discount for cash payment, so the couple put down $3000 toward a $4000 couch. The sofa would be custom produced, and it would take five weeks to deliver.

Six weeks after ordering, my friend called to find out what was the delay. It turned out the company had declared bankruptcy within those six weeks! He was out the entire $3000, with no legal leg to stand on... and definitely not a couch to sit on.

Now, if my friend had instead made his deposit with a credit card, he could have reported the transaction and had it canceled and refunded. But because he paid cash for his deposit, he became listed as one among thousands of creditors who could only expect to get pennies on the dollar returned to him after the bankruptcy. Maybe it would be enough to buy his wife apology roses when he tried to explain their gaffe.

Consumer vs. business protection for credit card usage

While ordering and paying for items using credit cards offers a layer of financial protection for consumers, it's important to understand the distinctions when credit cards are used for business purposes. The levels of protection are vastly different.

If I go into a shop and make a purchase using my business debit card, I only have a couple of days to dispute the charge. If instead I go into a shop and make the same purchase on my personal debit card, I can challenge the charge for 30 full days, or even several months.

The variations in allotted dispute time can make all the difference. As a young person, you may have established good habits of checking your bank statement and credit card statements once a month. As a consumer, this would typically allow you to catch any fraudulent activity within the allotted 30 days to file a charge dispute.

But if you're running a business, checking your account statements only once a month will never be enough. Fraudulent charges made at the beginning of your statement cycle might not be discovered for several weeks, and long before then, your ability to dispute them will have vanished.

Checking your bank and credit card statements

When reading your print or online bank statement and credit card statements, be aware that it's the little leaks that cause big problems.

It's often the little leaks that cause the biggest problems.

Perhaps you signed up for a monthly newsletter or service. There is a recurring charge associated with this purchase. Maybe you even subscribe to several such monthly services. When you first signed up, you might have thought, "Hey, it's only $97 a month to get all of this fabulous content." The ship sinks when you discover you have 5-7 of these recurring fees leaking from your account every month.

Any one of them would not be large enough to create a big ding on your wallet, but when you look at the bottom line on the statement, you now understand it could be a massive drain if left unchecked over time.

Now imagine if you aren't accustomed to checking your statements, even as much as once per month. After half a year you are surprised to discover your bank balance is lower than the gas tank after your teenager borrows the car for the weekend. Worse yet, when you finally examine the detritus of recent statements, you discover charges you don't even recognize.

Citibank hack

Many banks now offer apps you can use from your mobile device to monitor your account activity on the fly. However, pay special heed to where and how you acquire this app, explicitly following directions provided by your financial institution.

If you download an app from the Apple App Store, that software has been vetted to ensure it does not contain malware. However, the Google Play store did not always have such requirements. According to Minda Zetlin of creditcards.com, an app in 2010 became available that said it allowed Citibank users to check their accounts from mobile devices.

The first day it launched, it was downloaded by a large number of people who opened the app, typed in their username and password, but then experienced trouble getting into their account.

Some ignored it, assuming there were problems with a "beta" rollout. Others took action and called up Citibank saying, "I'm happy you have an app to check my account from mobile now, but when I put in my info, it didn't bring up my account."

You can imagine the shock on both sides of the phone when the company's response was, "Um... our app hasn't launched yet. It's still in testing and not estimated to release for another four weeks."[1]

The use of Multi-factor Authentication

Many banking apps now require two-factor authentication (2FA) or multi-factor authentication (MFA). You must still be vigilant because this process can be spoofed or hijacked to look like a business or organization needs to confirm credentials to use an app—and while you are working from a cell phone or typing quickly on a computer, you may not realize your data is being redirected to a site that is not valid, and is in fact being used to harvest credentials.

Along these same lines, be wary if you receive an email that says something like:

> Your account has been compromised.
> Please click on the link below to login.
> Answer these security questions
> to confirm the purchases were valid.

When people click on this link and type in their info, including data like their mother's maiden name or the last four digits of their Social Security number to "certify" their identities, what they have inadvertently done is provide access for criminals to commit further identity fraud.

Fraudulent charges

Whether or not you're aware, your entire financial profile can be purchased on the dark web... bundled with 9,999 other people's financial profiles. Information garnered can include things like your Social Security number, driver's license number, even health and medical record numbers as well as health insurance provider details.

Someone who has purchased such information can fraudulently charge a $95 procedure and then ask your insurance company to

---

[1] The full article can be accessed at: https://www.creditcards.com/credit-card-news/eight-tips-stop-banking-app-fraud-1282/.

reimburse the out-of-pocket expenditure. With 10,000 financial profile records, this same someone could open up 10,000 separate credit cards, perhaps buying $200 worth of gift certificates on each card. They might then go on to sell those gift certificates at discounted rates... separating themselves from later discovery once an investigation reveals the credit cards had been falsely created.

It doesn't even have to be a large amount to drain your bank account. In fact some of the most overlooked fraudulent activity happens at just $1–2 over months. This is the kind of under the radar activity no one will notice until or unless they go back and take a deep look at their statements.

Fraudulent charges can be small, but when spread across a large population, become lucrative for scammers.

Do you ever use a credit card at the gas station? If so, you may have noticed that they sometimes pre-charge your card to verify it before allowing you to pump your gas. The station charges a test amount, perhaps $1, then after you fill up, the $1 authorization gets released and the full amount gets charged.

But what happens when the station doesn't release that initial $1 authorization? It's too small an amount for most people to take action over, but if the station were to retain this $1... from everyone who used a credit card in a single day at the pump... now we're talking real money.

This same additive theory applies when thousands of credit cards are tapped for just $1 or $2 dollars a month. It's not enough to raise immediate red flags, but as any good matador knows, once the bull is angry and has his eye on you, the horns are sure to follow.

Even a *Shark* can be scammed

In business, charges can appear as perfectly legitimate transactions, only to be discovered as fraudulent activity several days or even weeks later. Depending on the nature and scale of your typical transactions, the amounts can become staggering, as *Shark Tank* judge Barbara Corcoran can attest. In addition to being a savvy real estate investor and joint-venture capitalist, Corcoran was the victim of a 2020 phishing scam that nearly landed a whale of a payout for its perpetrators.

As the former owner of a global real estate agency which she sold for $66 million in 2001, Corcoran is certainly no stranger to big-bucks investing, yet she and her staff still fell prey, as have more than 100,000 people who have reported being victims of this type of scam each year.

Phishing attacks are common methods of stealing usernames, passwords, and money. Hackers pretend to be a trustworthy source to convince you to share personal data. A scammer acting as Corcoran's assistant reportedly sent an invoice to her bookkeeper. The amount named was $388,700 for a renovation payment to one of Corcoran's property holdings. Because this Shark owned property in the location mentioned, the bookkeeper had no reason to be suspicious, and thus wired payment.

The problem was that the originating email address didn't actually belong to Corcoran's assistant. Instead, this scammer had set up an email account that was one letter different than the true assistant's. The mistake wasn't caught until the bookkeeper later emailed the assistant for a follow-up... using the correct email address.

"I really thought it was a goner," Corcoran told reporters. In a lucky twist, the German-based bank the bookkeeper used to wire the money was able to freeze the transfer before it was deposited into the scammer's bank account in China. This is highly unusual because most times once money is wired, it is immediately deposited. Frequently a scammer instantaneously transfers the money to a different account, making the path less traceable.

Always verify both the email address and ID of anyone to whom you send payments.

Last year, in 2020, the FBI received 23,775 complaints related to compromised business emails, with losses adding up to more than $1.7 billion. To avoid being taken in by this kind of fraudulent activity in your business, be sure to verify both the email address and identification of anyone to whom you send payments.

Signs, signs... everywhere there's signs

The Consumer Protection Act designates a window of 30 days to claw back payments made by a consumer using a credit card, however, remember business accounts will only have a 24-hour window. Although some banks may still help business owners recover fraudulent charges, they will not be required to do so by law.

Your awareness and monitoring of accounts is something you should not take for granted, especially if you hold accounts on other people's behalf. For example, one business I work with is a real estate attorney's office that routinely holds $200k-400k in escrow accounts on behalf of its clients. If these accounts get hacked and the escrow money is stolen, not only will the attorney have lost money that belongs to someone else, but may face legal charges of malfeasance from the bar as well as financial ramifications that may or may not be covered by a cyber security insurance policy.

Los Angeles-based real estate attorney Michelle Marsico lost $465k in 2010 at the height of the California housing market crash. On a day in which she had no incoming deposits or outgoing payments, she opted not to log in to check on the firm's bank accounts. Two days later when she discovered the missing funds, it was too late. A hacker who had gained access to Marsico's account numbers and online login credentials had already transferred funds and covered the digital paper trail.

Compounding the damage of fraudulent account hacking, most small businesses are unable to afford to pursue a lawsuit, and lawyers are reluctant to take on such cases because they are difficult to win and typically legal fees are not covered in any part of the rulings. Unfortunately, banking security has not kept pace with the availability of online account access, so business owners must vigilantly keep tabs on not only their own money, but on funds held in escrow on behalf of clients.

However, creative scammers can find ways to bypass even the most stringent business security measures. In the case of Long Island resident Cecilia Dowd, who was planning to buy her dream house in Glen Cove, an email purportedly from her attorney instructed her to wire the $504,350.89 balance to an escrow account. The next morning, she sent the money which included the majority of her life's savings as well as an inheritance. When she later discovered the email had come from an address just one character different than her attorney's legitimate account, the emotional toll of victimhood was almost as devastating as the financial loss itself.

In another example, prospective D.C. home buyers Sean Smith and Erin Wrona were asked to wire final payment to their title company in advance of closing on a five-bedroom house in Cleveland Park. When they later went to the title company's office to sign final paperwork, no one at the title company was even aware they had wired money... to the tune of $1.57 million.

In an age where identity fraud is commonplace, and the cash versus credit debate continues, it's little wonder that a number of individuals and organizations have sought out new ways to transact payments.

Alternate payment methods

PayPal, Venmo, Square, Point of Service devices, Google Pay, Apple Pay, Amazon Pay...

There are lots of different ways you can pay to play in today's modern world. You don't need to carry cash. You don't need a credit card. Heck, you don't even have to spend your Bitcoin or Dogecoin to buy that cup of coffee.

However, it's important to note that while many of these payment services are becoming ubiquitous—whether it's using your RF-enabled credit card for a half-caf latte at Starbucks, or tap-and-go at the gas station, or buying a subway ticket from your iPhone or iWatch—all of these services come with potential risk.

The ability to grab such information is not simple, but it's not as difficult as some might think. A properly equipped hacker can use a scanning device that fits in a spiralbound notebook or Marvel comic, or into a laptop case or even the shell of a cell phone carried outside their pocket. Then they walk down the street, skimming information from any device that's enabled with tap-and-go.

Luckily the advent of RFID-blocking wallets and purses have reduced the likelihood of data theft for those who adopt them.

The payment services themselves also offer a number of interesting warnings, such as "Never send or receive money from strangers." This includes organizations and even the payment portal itself, as hackers have sometimes impersonated a favorite charity or set up fake PayPal or Venmo sites. Be sure to report any payment requests from strangers, then also block the sender.

Much like a credit card, you should review your payments on a regular basis to ensure that a rogue payment, or multiple recurring payments, are not happening. You can also change the settings to only manually accept or send payments. It will require you to perform an extra step—which limits your ease of use—but that's the whole point of securing your payment method.

Consider using an RFID-blocking wallet or purse.

It is interesting to note, some of the services will allow you to dispute charges, and some will not. Just like personal and business credit cards offer different levels of protection, some services have a much shorter timeline to query or dispute a charge.

Note that Apple Pay transactions are explicitly stipulated to be matters between you and the merchant. Apple will not resolve the dispute for you. You have to take it up with your credit card company. Likewise, if you have a payment from Amazon, you may be able to dispute the charge—they have a very friendly service for this—but if they investigate and find no malfeasance took place, they can reinstate the charge very easily.

Also be aware that Amazon itself does not run their own credit card service. They use an outsourced group, similar to most of the big box stores, whether it be Costco or Walmart or Best Buy. Even though it is branded under the store name, it's really the third-party service that will review transactions. The best way to protect yourself is simply to keep an eye on your account, routinely reviewing transactions to ensure accuracy.

Also remember… there are scammers who will impersonate loved ones, maybe via text or email or phone, asking for assistance because they're traveling and in trouble or in jail. These con artists ask you to send money via Venmo, or even with credit card through PayPal or Apple Pay.

These alternate payment methods can normally make life easier, but by doing so, it also makes it much easier to get scammed. Be absolutely sure of the person or organization before automatically sending a payment.

Bitcoin and the cryptocurrency evolution

One of the reasons Bitcoin is so popular is that for vendors, there is no chargeback mechanism—unlike if you sell something and use PayPal to collect the money—where once the item is sold, PayPal is highly concerned with the customer's happiness so they can keep that person as a consumer. When a PayPal customer claims an item was never received, they will almost always receive a refund. This is a big issue for the merchant, who may now be out the physical item that's been sold, but also not receive payment. Bitcoin transactions do not have this forced refund mechanism.

American Express is also notorious for posting recharges after only one customer complaint, and with very little documentation to verify the validity of the customer claim. The vendor is responsible for eating that cost and associated product costs as well. And it's the same thing with Visa and Mastercard. It's the vendor who winds up covering each loss.

Another reason cryptocurrency (like Bitcoin) platforms work so well for vendors is that once there is an exchange, there is no "Right to Be Reimbursed." If I buy Product X from you and I pay via a Bitcoin transfer, but then later call you and want a return, the vendor can say, "Sorry, I don't know what you're talking about," and because it's a pseudo-anonymous currency, a refund does not have to be issued, though the vendor can choose to issue one.

A third reason Bitcoin became popular, especially for vice, is because there's no product listing that will appear on a credit card statement showing a purchase, for example, "2 lbs of weed" or "2 hrs of services" or "$500 to knock off grandma." Transactions to acquire drugs, prostitution, and even attempted murder for hire can take place in virtual anonymity—as detailed in the 2015 criminal sentencing of Ross Ulbricht, creator of the Silk Road black market. Using his site in conjunction with Bitcoin payment, anonymous customers and vendors bought and sold dangerous and addictive drugs with impunity. Ulbricht's billion-dollar platform, however, landed him a sentence for life in prison without the possibility of parole.

Cryptocurrency popularity

Though there are now more than 1600 cryptocurrencies in existence, including the most famous Bitcoin, one of the other popular ones started off as a joke—Dogecoin. Basically a tech writer was composing a piece about how easy and stupid it was to start your own cryptocurrency, so in December 2013 he used the image of the Shiba Inu dog from the "Doge" internet meme as its logo... thus Dogecoin. In May 2021 it had a $61 billion market cap, but it all started as a joke.

Corporations and other businesses are also trying to make money by creating their own cryptocurrencies. It's reminiscent of the Wild West when pioneers mined for gold with a pan in the river. But perhaps it bears even more similarity to a practice from the 1800s by which coal mines and lumber companies paid their employees in "scrip" rather than government-issued legal tender. These workers could then exchange their scrip in the company store for needed food and clothing—on which the employer had placed a large markup, thereby earning them an even larger profit. Unlike modern cryptocurrencies however, the scrip held no value whatsoever on the open market.

Cryptocurrency is like the Wild West, when pioneers mined for gold with a pan in the river.

How it started

When Bitcoin first came on the scene, people didn't "buy" coins, but rather "mined" them, using the extra CPU cycles of their computers.

By leaving the PC on overnight to run an installed piece of software, it could mine a coin over a few days.

The value back then was less than a cent apiece. The obvious problem of mining coins this way was that you were spending more on the electricity to mine the coin than what it was worth. It was like buying a 3D printer five years ago. It was pure geekdom.

But after a couple years, Bitcoin's value took flight. A famous meetup happened on the lower west side of Manhattan at Whole Foods. The attendees had a common seating area, and people would come to trade Bitcoin for actual dollars. You might go in, find somebody who wanted to sell to you, then you would download an app on your smartphone and physically give $20 to the scruffy Brooklyn bearded guy who was wearing socks and sandals, and he would deposit two Bitcoins into your electronic wallet.

Of course, you couldn't yet buy anything with this currency, but it was something that was interesting to have, and people were talking about it.

Who really benefits?

When even more people started writing and hearing about mining for Bitcoin, like any other good run-up, people began buying computer gear to get in on the game. The software for mining Bitcoin needed to use clock speeds that only a high-end graphic card could provide, because of the speed of screen refresh needed. What this really created was a run at the store on high-end graphic cards, typically required only for video gaming. Inventories depleted, then it became impossible to buy them.

Just like the Wild West, the people who made the most money were the ones supplying the mining equipment.

It got to a point where instead of being able to mine Bitcoin with any video gaming cards, it would take so long as it became more popular that people would buy or build special computer rigs to mine coins faster. It started out that with one megahash per second (MH/s) cycles, you could mine a coin in a day. Then you needed one gigahash (GH/s)—which is a thousand MH/s. Then you needed to get to twenty GH/s and on from there to terrahashes (TH/s).

The real people who benefited from this mania were the ones who sold the computer equipment. They would build these rigs and charge thousands of dollars—$15k, 20k, 30k—and those who were mining needed to have them with enough power and enough cooling... because these machines would run very hot. Now folks were spending money just to be able to make their money back.

When I first started looking at this phenomena, it reminded me of the 1849 Gold Rush. The place to make the money was *not* in the mining. The place to make the money was in selling tools and supplies— shovels, axes, tents, mining pans, lights, rope, dungarees. Levi Strauss got his start in 1853 in San Francisco, selling durable pants made out of tent canvas, then later switched to denim.

So who made the money in the Bitcoin mining era? It was the companies who promised that their computer hardware was going to be out in two weeks, or three weeks, or four weeks. But of course by the time their equipment rolled off the line, it was already too old to keep up. Serious "miners" needed newer and more powerful gear. But they had paid upfront for the hardware that was already obsolete—at least for the purpose of mining even a single Bitcoin.

Potential for loss

Like credit cards, cryptocurrencies have plenty of potential for loss. You will want to make sure that if you're holding money in any form, that you are storing it somewhere reputable. The U.S. Treasury has decided to tax cryptocurrency as regular income at this time. The tax implications are ever evolving and the most recent information can be found through irs.gov.

MT.GOX was a Bitcoin repository and trading site based in Japan that launched in July 2010. The name originated as an acronym for "Magic: The Gathering Online eXchange"—a card game exchange that later got repurposed as a Bitcoin trading post, and by 2014 it handled over 70% of the world's Bitcoin trades—almost as much fun for gaming nerds as seeing Dungeons & Dragons revived by Netflix's popular series *Stranger Things*.

The MT.GOX site was used as a cryptocurrency repository. When you own Bitcoin, your ownership is established by having it written in an electronic ledger multiple times to show that you own it or have transferred ownership. Ultimately, people wanted to take their holdings offline though, so they needed a wallet to store them. Fast forward from 2010 to 2014, and MT.GOX—a site that was not set up for high security, which had been trading the equivalent of bubble gum cards—morphed into a trading post for the equivalent of two- and three-carat diamonds.

Ultimately when MT.GOX got hacked, they lost about 50% of the Bitcoin they held for their customers. Because these transactions are non-reversible, the money was just gone. Proof of ownership in the ledger now showed that the account which had been hacked and picked up the coins had then distributed them to other accounts. Further, because the ledger didn't show who picked up the coins, when one account stole—sending to a thousand other accounts, from where they are then forwarded again—it "washed" the coin relatively quickly and became untraceable. At its peak price at the time of the hack, the stolen coin would amount to a value in excess of $17 billion.

Too good to be true

In late 2017, the value of a full Bitcoin soared from $1K up to $19K each. In April 2021, it peaked at $63K. Buying into Bitcoin became a mania, and otherwise rational people with a mortgage, two cars, and kids in college began taking out cash advances on their credit cards to purchase Bitcoin at these inflated rates... then taking out loans, and even second mortgages to buy more... because month over month the cryptocurrency was outperforming even the best stocks on the market.

Like any scam that seems too good to be true, it probably is.

Why do Ponzi schemes work? Why did Bernie Madoff succeed? Because people want easy money. People want to believe that what they're doing is smarter than the average bear. A Ponzi scheme, or confidence scheme, requires people to feel superior and more informed than their peers. They think, "I got a tip nobody else has... because I know the right people, I'm smarter, I work harder, I grease the right palms."

Just remember that those who benefit most from confidence schemes are the con men themselves. To be clear, I'm not saying Bitcoin is a Ponzi scheme. What I am saying is to be careful taking on debt to finance a rollercoaster ride of cryptocurrency speculation.

CHAPTER 3

PHISHING FOR GOLD

What is *phishing*? Phishing is basically the process where someone sends an email that looks like it's from a reputable company or a person in your contact list. The message is meant to induce you, the recipient, to reply with personal or sensitive information, or perhaps login credentials—essentially "fishing" for gold. It may link you to a site that looks like a valid company, perhaps Microsoft Office 365, to verify your username and password, but the font is a little bit off, or the URL is slightly wrong.

A phishing email may also appear to come from a company's CEO, addressed to the assistant-to-the-assistant comptroller of a mid-sized company. It looks like it came from the CEO's email address, but the CEO is saying that they are overseas, stuck someplace, and they need to have you wire $300,000 to them to get out of a bind. *"Just click on this link and it'll walk you through the steps you need to do."*

Similarly, *smishing* (SMS phishing) is where the same thing happens, but via text message. The message may originate from an unknown number and say something fairly innocuous like: "You've won a prize," or "Confirm your address for an Amazon delivery," or "UPS needs to confirm the time you'll be home." Then it provides a URL link.

Most large companies will either send a full link (where you can verify the domain) or perhaps they use a link-shortening device. The problem is that it can be difficult to determine which are valid and which are smishing. Only by hovering over the link, or sometimes actually following the link, can you know if it's a valid or invalid address. So, the rule of thumb is, if you do not usually communicate with the company or individual this way, then it is probably a setup.

It happens often in businesses where large sums of money are transferred around. A number of different insurance companies have had issues where claims adjusters have released tens of thousands (if not hundreds of thousands) of dollars, because a valid claim's information was intercepted prior to the insured receiving their money. Instead that claim money got diverted to a scam artist. The whole process of phishing relies on social engineering.

A sub-process of phishing is known as *spear phishing*, and is a targeted type of phishing where an individual is studied very, very closely. Their habits, foibles, and particular routine is scrutinized, and then a specially crafted email is sent to that individual, playing on certain aspects of their character.

Today's con artists are "phishing" for gold... your gold.

In our example above, the CEO emailed a third- or fourth-removed person from the CFO. This is often seen as somebody who has been stymied in their career, who hasn't received a promotion in a number of years. They have access to some funds in a corporate or small business environment, but they don't have the ultimate keys to the castle. Often, they may have access to five or six figures' worth of money. It might sound like it would be difficult to target somebody like this, but if you think about the number of posts where people gripe about work on social media, it's not that difficult to hone in on disgruntled employees. Then these spear phishers craft very specific, tailored phishing emails to the employee—to give a sense of importance, making the employee feel recognized and trusted with a big responsibility, inducing them to release some of the gold from the coffers.

Let's look closer at some common phishing expeditions.

The Nigerian Prince email

This classic fraud starts with someone claiming to be royalty from some third-world country. It comes in a variety of forms, but basically says, "Hello friend, I'm reaching out to you as a trusted mutual colleague suggested you might be able to help me. While working in the ministry office of the oil fields of Nigeria, I found a loophole and

I was able to hide away some money. I've converted this money into (currency) and it's sitting in my bank account (safety dep box). I know I can trust you. Our mutual friend says you are very discreet."

...Of course you get to keep the other 10% as a commission.

The whole idea relies on the greed of the email recipient. The claim is made that as a "Nigerian prince" (or another prince of a country far away), "I am one of 100 sons," or "The money was given to me in a secret way," or "I am fleeing the country." The claim ends with "It's only safe if I take it out of a U.S. bank."

This is a traditional short-con where they ask for some personal information to transfer money into your account. "All I need to proceed is the name of your bank, your account and routing numbers, and I can proceed with the deposit, and sign this document" (or they lift your signature). On the short-con, they take this information and remove money from your account immediately.

As mentioned, they are playing on the principle of greed.

On a long-con version, they deposit a sizeable amount of money, maybe $5000, into your account, maybe once, maybe twice. Then over time, they determine how much money you have in this account, and then all at once they make a massive withdrawal.

It plays on the "I've got an inside guy... someone who's taking care of me" personality trait. People who are scammed by this believe they are good people, smart people, lucky people... and they also believe they are entitled to an easy windfall.

A variation

An industry variation includes the "I-know-what-you-did-last night in your hotel" email. This scam is all about protecting your assets. It's more often than not an overreaction.

In this example, the email implies the sender has video clips of something you purportedly viewed on your computer, paired in tandem with video of you watching this salacious goody. Then the sender offers you one or more "solutions" to spare your reputation, usually involving payment made in an untraceable manner like a Bitcoin or other cryptocurrency transfer.

Here's another "I'll scratch your back…"

In this email scam, a stranger reaches out to you from what they claim to be a position of authority in a foreign country. When you reply with your bank account information so they may "entrust you" with their business funds, instead of filling your account with their country's massive treasure, they instead make a hasty withdrawal and fill their own coffers with your hard-earned moolah.

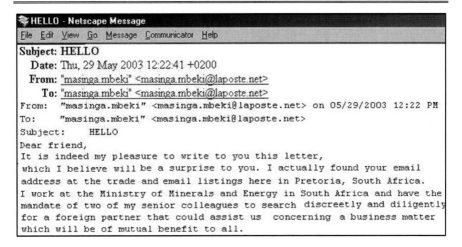

Smishing

In some cases, rather than pretending to be a delivery company or prize-granting opportunity, the text message will play on urgency and your fear of loss to induce you to click on a bogus link.

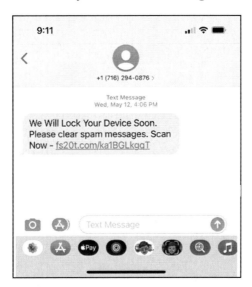

Locking up your gold — Beware of ransomware

Yes, it's morally and ethically wrong for someone to access your data and lock you out from being able to retrieve or restore it to your computer. But it's neither expensive nor difficult for someone to do this. If you want to avoid falling prey to these scammers, you need to protect yourself before such an event occurs.

What does it look like when your files have been ransomed? Well, it can look like differently for different people. You might go to open a file and instead you get an error message that says: "The file doesn't exist" or "The file type is not valid." Or perhaps instead of having a .doc or .docx file extension, it shows something like ".cj714432" and all the folders inside that folder also now have the same extension... except for one which shows a .txt extension.

When you open this .txt file, it'll be written in almost good English.

> "You may wonder what's going on. We have taken over your computer. You have 2 days from [DATE] to deposit $10k to this account [flijweriwet9323 with URL and instructions so you can bypass your company firewall]."

Most times ransomware will not damage the OS files, so you can reboot your computer, but still you won't be able to do anything with it. The ransomware thieves have encrypted your data but not rendered your computer useless.

Often this .txt file will even contain a "Support Phone Number" so you can contact them. You might begin to believe your computer has been ransomed by some highly elaborate organization, but it could just be some kid in Iowa or South Korea who's running a bot. Or it could be the mob in Trenton. Who knows? But they frequently have a contact point or support number to speak with someone who can walk you through how to pay the ransom and regain access to your files.

Most of these scammers are good about un-encrypting your files after you have paid their demands... because they are trying to function as a business and they want to make money. If enough people have ransomware computer files and *don't* release them after paying, then people will stop paying.

How can this happen in the first place?

Perhaps you have received an email that tells you: "Your account has been hacked. I have been watching you, and I know all about the videos you've been watching. If you don't want me to tell everyone about your filthy little habits, then..."

It's all based on social engineering and the fear of loss—the perceived potential for loss and how afraid you are of the consequences.

So you've received a SMShing text. Now what?

Check the link that you are being asked to open. If the text is from FedEx or Costco or Walmart, what address is it trying to send you to? Companies will almost always direct you to their own websites, not a third-party domain name. If it looks fishy, do not click on it. Contact the company that the text is supposedly coming from. However, use their known website or phone number, *not* the website or number that is provided in the text message.

If it looks fishy...
DO NOT CLICK
ON IT!

When you get a clear SMShing text, first and foremost, do not open the link that is contained in the text. Clicking on this link can result in malware or malicious software being installed on your phone or tablet.

You can block numbers being used to send these texts. You can also block texts from unknown or unverified senders. Your wireless provider can do this for you, or you can do it yourself on your phone directly. You can also use call blocker apps, which vary by phone type and carrier.

Additionally, you can report these messages as SPAM through processes provided by your wireless carrier, or forward the message to 7726 (SPAM) and you can also report the actor to the Federal Trade Commission at ReportFraud.ftc.gov.

The more frequently these types of SPAM and SMShing texts are sent on to the FTC and your phone carrier, the quicker this type of annoying and problematic social engineering hijacking will be blocked and cleaned up.

CHAPTER 4

BEWARE OF SOCIAL TRIGGERS

What makes people tick? This is the question social engineers work to figure out and then manipulate. All human beings become socialized to their environment as they grow from infant to toddler to child and on up to adulthood. Social norms become internalized. We learn to navigate a crowded corridor or street without bumping into other people. We say, "Bless you," even when the person sneezing is a complete stranger. We press the elevator button even though it is already lit and three other people are waiting.

Shorthand phrases and actions also become automatic—it's "soda" in the northeast, but "pop" in the Midwest. These automatic actions and reactions—and the jarring feeling when the expected reaction does not happen—break us out of the stupor as we strive to accomplish daily tasks.

But a social engineer will work to slip in between the expected, automatic responses and tread lightly to not create that jarring reaction that invites scrutiny. All in the pursuit to find out what makes us tick...

What is Social Engineering?

Social engineering is the psychological manipulation of people to gain confidential information or access to resources and information. It can be used to trigger someone into taking an action outside the norm... like when your teenager takes out the trash without being asked, then hits you up for $100.

One example of social engineering would be a psychic (not a real psychic, obviously) who uses open-ended questions in a large-group format to identify potential "marks," thus proving their psychic ability by asking leading questions like: "Has anyone recently lost a loved one," or "Is anyone having trouble with teenage children?"

These are questions to which many would instantly respond: "Yes! You know me so well." Then by reading verbal and nonverbal reactions, the so-called psychic can solicit more and more clues and data, which lead to a level of trust and sharing that would be otherwise impossible to obtain quickly.

A more malevolent social engineer might target the receptionist at a doctor's office—the gatekeeper to an awful lot of confidential information. Someone who has done reconnaissance work may discover that a drug rep routinely visits this office once a week on Thursday afternoons. That person might then call in to the receptionist shortly after the drug rep would've departed and say something like, "Hello, Sally. This is so-and-so. I must have dropped my car keys while I was there... can I come look for them?" Or this person might ask for clarification about an order that was just placed, phishing for more detailed information from the receptionist.

Even teenagers know how to employ social engineering...
like when they take out the trash, unasked, then hit you up for $100.

The origins of social engineering can be traced to the biblical story of Isaac and his two sons, Jacob and Esau. For those who are not up on their Sunday School reading, Isaac was preparing to die, and was set to offer the firstborn son Esau his birthright. Isaac asked Esau to prepare his favorite meal of a lamb stew. While Esau went out to begin, Jacob and his mother launched a different plan.

By modern standards, you might compare Esau to Arnold Schwarzenegger's dashing and strong character in the movie *True Lies*, while Jacob would've been the geek in the back room. Esau was big, Jacob was little. Esau was hairy. Jacob had no beard. Esau could hunt. Jacob could not.

Being the second son, who would not inherit, Jacob was encouraged by his mother Rebekah to take his brother Esau's place and try to obtain the inheritance that Isaac was about to bestow. So Jacob made a lamb stew that his mother helped him prepare, then dressed in his brother's finest clothes and further disguised himself by placing lamb skin on his forearms and neck. Then he brought the stew into his father's tent.

Isaac, old, dying and mostly blind, smelled the stew and called to his son, "Esau, come closer." Jacob brought the stew to his father and his father smelled and tasted the stew and was happy, so he asked his son, "Come closer."

Isaac reached out and felt the "hairy" arms and neck of his son, and knew that it was Esau. Isaac asked his son to speak, and when Jacob spoke, his voice didn't match Esau's, but since all the other senses told Isaac that Esau was standing before him, Isaac mistakenly bestowed Esau's birthright onto Jacob. This actually resulted in a great deal of trouble and strife between the descendants of Jacob and the descendants of Esau—the Muslims and Jews.

The reason why this is an excellent example of social engineering is that Jacob used multiple reinforcing methods to trick his father into believing Jacob was someone he was not. It was a rich and layered deception that caused a person who had a slight doubt to instead rely on all the other proofs in front of him, to overlook his doubts and concerns by virtue of the fact that Isaac could not see. In doing this, Jacob gained access to the resources of the family to which he otherwise would've been denied.

A modern-day rip-off occurred in the UK when a woman received a call from someone purporting to be her cell phone provider. They told her she was late with a 60£ payment, and so she used her debit card to authorize a transfer of funds to cover what she "owed."

Less than ten minutes later, she received a call from the fraud team at her bank. She had been scammed. They encouraged her to transfer funds to a new account since her debit card was directly linked to her previous bank account.

They talked her through the process of logging in online and making multiple transfers of less than 9,000£ into this new account. As each deposit cleared, they would tell her when to transfer the next amount.

Unfortunately for this woman, it was a double scam. The second (and larger) theft was enabled by the fear triggered in the victim through the first thief's actions.

Physical access in a digital age

During Cold War struggles between the U.S. and then Soviet Union, an example of social engineering using technology took place. As with all such schemes, this one relied on gaining someone's trust using enough kernels of truth that it caused the "mark" to put aside any doubts and cooperate willingly. In 1962, the photocopying industry was dominated by Xerox—an American-based company. Despite the military and political rivalry between the two countries, every single photocopy made by U.S.S.R. consulates and other offices inside the Soviet republic itself were made on Xerox machines.

The only way organizations and companies could use photocopiers at that time was to purchase such machines along with a service contract that would routinely bring in a licensed repairman to provide maintenance and service.

CIA officials approached Ray Zappoth, a 36-year-old mechanical engineer for Xerox, about creating a bug that would allow the U.S. to garner intel secretly. By playing on the social engineering trigger of patriotic duty, the CIA used Zappoth's and Xerox's technology to help gather information that could be used against the adversary.

A camera system was developed and installed on the Xerox photocopiers that could store images of every document that passed through the machine. These systems would fill up fairly quickly, and when the Xerox reps would return to the offices on a routine two-week time frame to service the machines, they would clean the copier and reconfigure it. Meanwhile one of the service tech's tasks was to swap out the camera with a new one, then return the film for processing and analysis by U.S. intelligence.

Oddly enough, Zappoth suggests that due to the number of surveillance camera parts ordered from Xerox after this invention, he believes the technology may have been used to spy on U.S. allies as well as its enemies.

In this way, a needed piece of technology—a photocopier that had a required maintenance schedule—was used to acquire strategic and confidential data. While this is an interesting Cold War spy story, what may be less well known is that anyone walking into a building wearing a repair tech's uniform and carrying a clipboard and tool bag is likely to gain access to most offices located in that entire building.

A frequently occurring example, the "technician" in uniform approaches the receptionist. *"Someone called about a problem with the photocopier?"* Very rarely does the person at the front desk answer, "No," because most businesses have frequent problems with photocopiers. In large offices, it's very conceivable someone on staff placed such a service call.

As most pieces of equipment now, these photocopiers and printers are part of the office computer network, and it becomes very easy for the "technician" to add some sort of monitoring system that will provide a physical entry point into a network that may have otherwise been well guarded if they used technology and digital safeguards.

In a 2007 cyber security investigation, a financial institution hired Steve Stasiukonis to ascertain whether the business's employees were so accommodating and service-oriented that it would allow their network to be infiltrated. One branch office turned him away, but a second allowed him direct access to the photocopier where he plugged his laptop into their network. Under the ruse of "validating" that the printer would work properly from company computers, several employees fell for his ruse and let him plug in a U3 USB memory stick (a tool that is designed to launch portable Windows applications from the USB stick without prompting) to their machines, which could quickly and untraceably copy data files.

After the events in late 2001, it is no longer possible for an outsider to walk into most office lobbies in New York City and go straight to an elevator without some form of identification validation. However, as the popular TV show *Burn Notice* highlighted, walking into a place of business confidently in a service uniform, especially with an inside contact in the building—or when someone has done extensive research—a person can gain access to most office buildings in almost any midsize or large city. Office security is often fairly lax without even a sign-in or identification validation procedure.

What to watch out for

Such a "technician" might use social engineering to discover a doctor's office has two receptionists—one who is a savvy twenty-five-year-old who asks to see everyone's credentials and work orders before allowing entry to the building, and the other who has been working for this doctor for thirty years and feels comfortable and confident. When they learn the office always uses Acme Pro to service their photocopier, they will want to make their approach when the older receptionist is on duty—wearing Acme Pro uniforms since this will increase their chance of success.

By observing social media posts of the gatekeepers, these outsiders learn firsthand about the types of problems, fears, and concerns faced in the industry. They will then call or email—perhaps even write a physical letter—with a message that addresses those specific concerns.

One way this activity can sneak in is through an invitation that asks the worker to take action and inspires them by creating an urgent incentive offer that has an expiration date. It might be an online survey, filling out a form, or subscribing to an online group... and if they take action within the designated period of time, they will get a bonus—that the outsider knows will be valued, because they've done their research—perhaps a $10 gift certificate to the coffee shop down the road, or a 15% off coupon for a favorite nail salon.

By designing FOMO (fear of missing out) into the bonus, in exchange for handing over information that would typically not be seen as very valuable, these outsiders create an incentive to fill out a form or take a survey. That form or website may contain malware or a trigger mechanism, or a follow-up thank you gift might be physically mailed, such as a USB drive

FOMO =
Fear of Missing Out

they can plug in to store all their photos. Once connected to the office computer, it gives the outsiders broader access to the entire network.

In an article from April 9, 2020, Security Boulevard's Casey Crane posits a more immediately intrusive data breach. "Tina" in Accounts Payable receives a call from "Drew" who represents one of the company's vendors. Drew alerts her there was an issue with the most recent payment. His company recently changed banks and updated info was sent to all the clients, but Tina's company and one other did not update the account info properly.

Drew is friendly, confident, and charming, while Tina is embarrassed for the oversight. Drew sends her an email with the updated banking information and says he'd be really grateful if Tina can go ahead and make the payment ASAP so the company's service won't lapse.

Tina immediately opens the email, which has arrived as Drew promised, and she processes the payment to rectify the situation. But when the boss discovers the discrepancy two weeks later and informs Tina that a data breach has been traced back to her workstation, not only has she authorized a fraudulent payment, but she's opened up her company's IT network to a hacker.

The point is, creating this FOMO-must-act-now incentive can be used for both good and ill. It creates a sense of urgency that gets people to take action... even when taking action may not be in their best interest.

Everybody's watching

So far we've spoken about how gaining physical access can compromise a physical or digital network. Similarly there have been a number of reports about people hiding small cameras in restrooms—a place normally considered fairly secure—in order to record possible conversations and activities that could provide information to legitimize social engineering scams.

In Christopher Hadnagy's 2010 book, *Social Engineering: The Art of Human Hacking,* he tells of an audit he performed at a theme park that sold tickets online. With his kids, he approached the one lady manning a computer at the ticket window. He told her his daughter saw their ad in a restaurant and they bought the tickets online with the discount code, but when the hotel printer was on the fritz, he saved them as a PDF instead. "Could I just log in or have you log in to my email to get the document?"

Sure enough the employee clicked on the PDF which launched a malicious piece of code that was scripted to give him access to her computer and start auto-collecting data.

He presented the company with a recording of the conversation, detailing the method used and the heart strings that were pulled. This kind of (painfully revealing) audit helped to educate the company so such an attack could not be repeated, costing it thousands or more dollars over time.

Remember, access to a space may not be limited to just network access. Cameras and recording devices could be rigged to transmit to outside monitors, and then in turn used to steal corporate secrets.

In the 1987 movie *Wall Street,* Charlie Sheen's character tries to obtain insider trading info by landing a job with the agency that cleans a law office's space after hours. As a foreman, he is granted free range to walk around the office—including access to file cabinets, papers on the desks, as well as the desks themselves.

By now you should be easily able to understand that given enough time and energy, someone could use this and other social engineering techniques to gain leverage and perhaps harm a rival business.

Creating urgency

A first connection allows someone to gain physical access. This is the wedge or foot in the door that will later be leveraged to create a bigger fissure. Early pieces of information this outside source will be looking for includes the receptionist(s)'s first name(s), knowing who might answer phone calls, and what hours that person works. Such a person will want to learn what the receptionists look like physically, and perhaps troll them through social media pages.

Most of that information is not protected, but it gives the outsider insight into what makes these gatekeepers tick. It can also provide detailed knowledge of what triggers these receptionists, which can often be used as a leverage point for blackmail or enlisting the receptionist in illegal activity.

This is the quintessential *Oceans 8* scene. Access is gained to a video camera designer's computer so they can see the security camera layout at a facility. The "villains" discover the designer is single and loves a particular breed of dog, so they create a malicious Facebook site that specifically targets this person. By clicking a single link through that site, the designer starts a chain reaction of events that downloads malware onto his computer.

This is a very elaborate example, but it's important to note that if someone wants to gain access to the low-hanging fruit of your personal or company data, it can be done, so we must stay knowledgeable and strengthen our security in both physical and digital ways in order to stay safe.

Beware of sites that ask you to sign in using your credentials from another site, such as Facebook or Google. If you are required to enter your credentials on a portal, even if it looks like Google or Facebook, you may be passing your username and password directly to the scammer.

Family connection

Why do older people fall for scams? Stereotypically, it's because they're less tech savvy than their younger counterparts, and while that's sometimes true, it's not always the case. Just as often it may be because they're lonely and afraid of loss. They also usually have more free time on their hands.

Older people are frequently the targets of financial scams.

A 2018 *Security Through Education* blog by Ryan MacDougall details an area of elder fraud he calls "vishing"— voice phishing. Common schemes include lottery phone scams, grandparent scams, and romance scams. He encourages the public to request information about the caller—company name, callback number, website—and to take the time to validate the identity. All of these actions delay the attack and can allow time for critical thinking to help someone assess whether the request is legitimate.

Lonely elders are more likely to be vulnerable to someone who calls and invites them into a conversation. This act of paying attention will have created reciprocity... simply by listening to them. It's a trait that's ingrained in us as individuals. When we feel we owe another person something, or that we might disappoint this nice person—the one we want to continue being our "friend"—it creates a fear of future abandonment.

For example, if a person has not heard from their adult son or daughter in a long time, and a scammer calls, impersonating that child, it can happen that the older person will develop a fear of losing this connection to their "child." Sooner or later there's a money request, small enough it doesn't seem unusual. But over time those money requests gets bigger. When the scammer later says they have to go on an important trip (or the hot water heater broke, or the car died)... and they need money... the parent's heart strings may be pulled to offer this "child" the needed resources.

Other family connections

From a safety perspective, there are tons of email scams about relatives. One might begin: "Hi Grandma, I'm in prison. I was taking a trip to Mexico for the semester." Or sometimes it's a phone call: "I don't want to tell Mom or Dad. Can you help by sending money?"

The desire to help a grandchild is strong, especially if the scammer has done some research and knows there are tense relationships between child and parent. The grandparent may be softened enough to want to help even more because of this.

Another scarier version might include a kidnap threat, and often it feels safer to pay the ransom demand than to reach out to the police and use a hostage negotiator.

When Mark Walker received a call from his daughter, he answered immediately. But it was not his daughter. Instead it was a man claiming to have kidnapped his daughter. He told Walker he'd murder the daughter if Walker did not send ransom money.

Beware of scammers impersonating a family member or loved one.

"He said, 'I'm not playing around'," Walker told an NBC affiliate in Indianapolis. "He said, 'If you call the police I'm going to kill her'."

While Walker felt scared, he did not give into the caller's demands. He asked his wife to check on his daughter. She was safe. Walker was a victim of what's known as *virtual kidnapping*, a hoax that is spreading, according to the FBI.

Three recommended ways to protect yourself from such a hoax:

- Develop a family "safe word" – Ask the kidnapper to have your child relay the family safe word to verify they've been taken. Most of the time this will reveal the ruse.

- Contact the reported victim – As you keep the person talking, reach out to your loved one by email or text. Because the scammer is only faking the Caller ID and does not have the victim's actual phone, your loved one can respond.

- Stall – Keep the caller talking, ask them to slow down and repeat themselves, ask if you can call them back. As soon as you can ascertain the safety of your loved one, the scam falls apart.

How to spot a scam

There are hundreds of these kinds of scams running around on a regular basis. To protect yourself, here are top tips to recognize when you are being targeted.

1) Where is the call originating?

Check the incoming number. Is it coming from your area code if it is a personal call? Is it coming from a blocked number? Is it coming from a relative or known number, or from an unknown number?

2) What email address is this really coming from?

Hover over the email with your cursor to see if the address it appears to be coming from is where it says it's from.

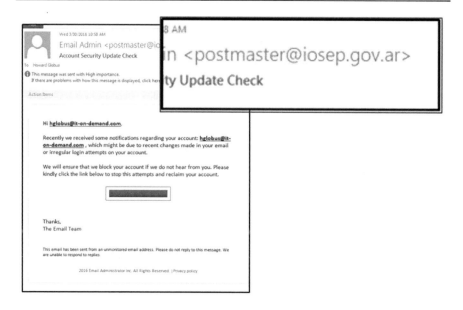

If you look closely at the address, you'll see the ".ar" indicating it originates in Argentina. Since I have not sent emails to or through Argentina, I was automatically suspicious. The site, iosep.gov.ar, is a valid Argentina site (or so it appears).

However, when I right-click the URL to grab the link it actually wants to send me to, I discover it's a site based in Mauritania.

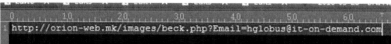

The .mk extension is what points to Mauritania. And it is unlikely that Argentina would then be sending my traffic on to Mauritania.

If I go to the website (without passing my credentials or the subfolders) of orion-web.mk, I get to this website:

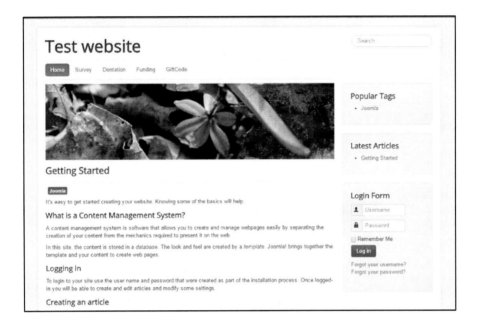

If I further go to the website (without allowing my email address to be used to pre-populate the page), I get this warning from Google Chrome that the address is a known phishing site.

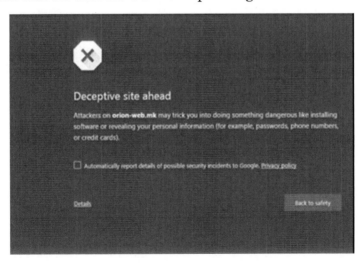

When I continue on, it looks like a valid login page for a stripped down webmail platform running on a Linux or Windows server using a cPanel interface. Notice that there is no email address to enter with the password.

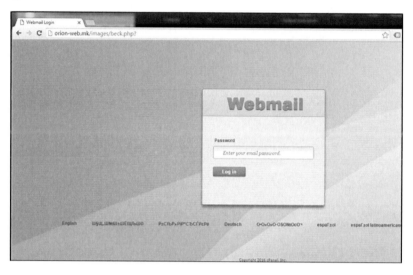

If I instead give it a bogus email address by substituting that for mine in the original link, it enters this new address and again asks for a password.

http://orion-web.mk/images/beck.php?
Email=WhoSaysWeShouldNotGoHere@gmail.com

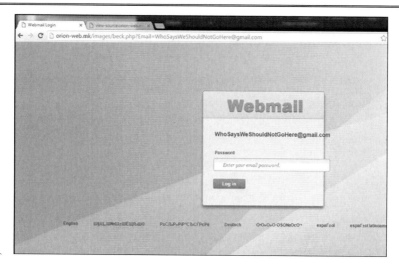

For my bogus address I enter a bogus password and they offer me "additional 100 GIG upgrade." There are several red flags now. Gigabytes of storage should be abbreviated as "GB," not GIG. The grammar of "Your mailbox quota have been" is atrocious, the word "scheduled" is misspelled, and the statement ends in not one but two periods. Had I given my correct email address and password, my mailbox would now be compromised.

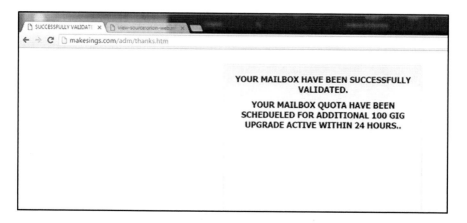

So far, it's seemed like this scam is originating from Argentina, and then Mauritania, however, when I view the code behind the "login page," I can spot the original code is coming from a .ru address, which is Russia. The entirety of the code on the page is about 922 lines and bounces us around to a bunch of different countries and locations.

Please be cautious before you enter your email address, password or other sensitive data that may result in compromising your computer, your email account, your bank account or your credit card accounts.

3) Does the spelling and/or grammar sound right? Is this how the person normally communicates?

The following examples highlight clues of spelling and grammar that may alert you to a scam.

Due to Equifax' s latest **security breach**, your current TransUnion, Equifax, and Experian scores may have changed.

Â
Â
Your Scores are available now at no charge.
Â

View Your Score

Over 500,000 Customers - A Brand You Can Trust. Completely Discreet. Order Online Now.

Your Prescription ED Medication Delivered To Your Doorstep.Discreet Packaging & Delivery.Free Consultation. Completely Confidential.Effective in 80% of Men with Erectile Dysfunction

https://linkprotect.cudasvc.com/url?a=http%3a%2f%2fluxstockeve nt.su%2f%3fqazwsodenVTyvwyTCDRXRwsgvgvDRYReewYFfctfcR DDYXRX&c=E,1,aq2hI9iAD1CTlJcmWVDQ6FwTUYpiJQttQTHRji 2heZ_L6TqEKQIRBxcpFJR_w9NZ1W1S4E-t1AfPH-AWVom1boqvDTrxSruOIx3ykazcl13Xt9NoXjn_b-icEw,,&typo=1

IMPORTANT DOMAIN SEO NOTIFICATION
Notification Purchase Offer, 08.08.2020

Domain: Bxxxxxt.Com
Expiration: 19.05.2020

In this latter case, you can be suspicious because of the European date format used in an email purportedly from the U.S.

Another trick to ascertain whether an email is part of a phishing scam is to copy/paste portions of the email into an internet search engine.

Frequently someone else will have already received a similar scam and posted it online to debunk it for the sake of others.

Foreign-language example

A 2018 New York City telephone scam actually targeted Chinese families. When the call was answered, a recorded message speaking in Mandarin said, "Your visa is about to be revoked and you need to return to China. Your loved one is in danger. If you send $$ to this particular address..."

Anyone who does not understand the language will simply hang up, but it's a very powerful trigger if you are a Chinese immigrant. In response, many have sent millions of dollars to these scammers posing as members of the Chinese consulate.

Domestic Robo-calling

Another type of recorded message that might greet you when you pick up the phone is: "This is the United States Social Security Office calling." The automated message says YOUR NAME, and adds, "You are about to have a penalty levied against you. Call this number back right away to make arrangements." You can hear a recorded example at: https://www.consumer.ftc.gov/blog/2018/12/what-social-security-scam-sounds.

The first clue that something is not right (if you weren't aware of such scams to begin with) is that federal agencies do not phone people regarding problems. Letters are sent. And then certified letters follow.

> SCAM ALERT:
> *Federal agencies will never phone you regarding problems.*
>
> (IRS, Social Security, FBI)

If you go so far as to call the number back, your call will be answered live. For those of you who have ever had to deal with the Social Security department—or really most government agencies—you will realize that *never* happens.

A second clue will be that someone with a distinctly foreign accent will answer your call, claiming their name is something like "Dave Smith" or "Ron Johnson" or some other simple Anglicized name.

Perhaps they will even choose the name of someone famous. When you ask them to confirm that you heard correctly, they will simply say, "Yes, that's my real name."

Another clue, if you are aware to listen for it, is that most agents of the federal government will share their badge number or an ID number of some sort. These phone scammers will provide no such identification. They will tell you that you owe some amount of money, and instead of being able to take payment from you over the phone by a check or credit card, they will instead ask you to pay by Bitcoin or to purchase gift cards and read them the code on the back.

You might be surprised to learn that this scam actually works, but if it didn't, then these scammers would not continue, would they? The con artists on the phone make threats like: "Unless you comply, a warrant will be issued for your arrest." Or "The police have been called and are on their way. We can stop their arrival by taking care of this over the phone." So, yes, people will go out and purchase gift cards to give to the scammers on the phone, because they're concerned they will be sent to jail, or suffer some other horrible fate.

SCAM ALERT: *Payment requests via gift cards*

These fake "government reps" will even curse at you, which is not something any government agency member should ever do. If in fact you call them back at the number provided and suggest to them that it's a scam, they will curse at you again and hang up. However, if you should be persistent and call them back two or three or more times, the number will get disconnected. *Ask me how I know.*

These are security FOMO abandonment methodologies, and they rely heavily on our socially ingrained psychological reactions.

In his book, *Influence: The Psychology of Persuasion,* Robert Cialdini talks about the "recordings" in our brain and how certain triggers automatically trip us up. He calls them "shortcuts" and suggests we create such pathways to get by in culture, indeed, even to get by as human beings.

He explores the psychology behind why people say "yes" and make predictable actions. For example, if an individual standing on the

Serengeti Plains sees an object charging toward him, he might immediately make an assessment of the danger and do a front-of-the-mind calculation about whether there is danger. Cialdini argues this individual will not react quickly enough to remove himself from danger... thus taking himself out of the gene pool. An individual in same situation who instead *runs* is much more likely to survive and therefore remain in the gene pool.

These automatic processes are what allowed our ancestors to survive in life. Modern equivalents include routine tasks like crossing the street, checking traffic lights, assessing traffic patterns, and pushing a baby carriage while talking to a neighbor or friend. These have all become unconscious behaviors, because as humans we couldn't possibly make all these calculations and still get everything done in a day.

Con artists in film

I love movies, and I love both short cons and long cons in movies. Possibly my favorite is the 2001 film *Heist,* in which Gene Hackman plays a long con within a long con, within another long con.

In the 1990 movie, *Grifters,* we enjoy seeing how some people actually want to be conned. They want to get something for nothing and they want to feel like they are on the inside. To maintain this feeling, they will be willing to forego something they want in order to get and stay on the inside. The problem is they don't realize they're the mark, rather than being in on the game.

Pulling the levers

In a nutshell, social engineering allows outsiders to learn what triggers you and then pull your levers like a master manipulator, only with more malevolent outcomes. While you might be glad that Facebook offers you a perfectly targeted t-shirt in your size and favorite color showing off the month in which you were born, you would be less thrilled if—when you scrolled past that offer—the next ad cursed at you and threatened to kidnap your child unless you purchased the item.

Be careful to whom you grant authority and trust.

CHAPTER 5

OUT-OF-THE-BOX VULNERABILITIES

A network device is very much like a car. When first purchased and driven off the lot, a car customer will expect the vehicle to have had its oil topped up, radiator fluid mixed, windshield washer fluid filled, tire pressure optimized, and so forth. However, anyone who expects to drive a car off the lot for 50k miles without doing basic maintenance or adding gasoline would be deemed quite silly. Clearly the car needs fuel to run, and the engine needs fresh oil to properly function. When a tire looks low, it needs to be inflated.

However, many people feel that when they buy a computer or a piece of network gear like a switch or a wireless access point, they can take it out of the box, plug it in, and let it run and never have to think about it again.

A simple internet search can reveal default User IDs and passwords for most if not all networking gear—things like the lowest-end home network switch to the state-of-the-art Cisco router, wireless printers, wireless access points, multi-function copiers found in small offices and large corporations, firewalls and all kinds of things that have a plug or a wireless connection to attach to a network in your home or office. Too many customers fail to change this default User ID and password, practically painting a bullseye target and inviting hackers to take aim.

In the last couple of years, internet service providers have become more clever, trying to assist such users. When their representative installs a router or modem in your home or office, they may set up an ID and password that's randomized and printed on the device, rather than a default code anyone can find on the internet.

But you should still beware. If this ID and password are printed on the device, anyone who has physical access to your space can copy and/or use it. Also, there will still be generic backdoor passwords so customer service and technicians can access the device to help you when there are problems. These backdoor passwords are often readily available, again using a well-crafted internet search.

Are you a target?

So how can your computer or network be accessed and how can your network be vulnerable? There are four primary ways this happens:

1) You are onsite and someone is trying to access your device remotely.

   Perhaps you work from home, or stay at home the majority of the time. It could also happen after malicious malware is downloaded and installed while a hacker is doing a network search on IP addresses and happens to stumble on yours.

2) You are onsite and the person trying to access the device is also onsite.

   You may have a technician or repair person come onsite. Perhaps you have invited a houseguest that stays overnight. Or maybe a friend of your child or spouse is visiting and didn't like what you served for dinner.

3) You are not onsite and the person is remote.

   This could even happen while you are at work and no one is home. If someone is scanning for open IP addresses, they may discover yours in a scenario similar to #1 above.

   Or you might be away on vacation for an extended period of time and your information becomes available because someone posted what they gathered while doing open IP address scans or on a hacking site like in scenario #2 above.

4) You are not onsite but the person is onsite.

   Perhaps you have been at work for a period of time while some reconnaissance was done by the other person to learn approximately how long the house would be empty. The culprit may be casing your network, similar to planning for a burglary— someone coming onsite, possibly taking physical material, installing software or gaining access to the network while onsite.

Alternatively you may be away on vacation and there is an extended period of time where access can be gained to the local network.

In all these scenarios, the attacker may be using open-source info on how to access common consumer-grade products that are in use in the home. Linksys, NETGEAR, and low-end Cisco wi-fi routers have standard usernames and passwords on the devices. These are quite easy to find based on a Google search by model number.

Network switches from DLink, NETGEAR and the like also have generic standard usernames and passwords. If you want to change these default usernames and passwords but have lost your documentation or forgotten how, an article by Peter Selmeczy provides instruction at: https://proprivacy.com/guides/default-router-login-details.

Computer and network equipment need regular updates and security patches to keep your data secure.

What large businesses know is that their network equipment needs to be maintained on a regular basis. That means changing default generic passwords and sometimes even usernames, regularly checking for updates and security patches, making time to apply and test those patches, and to examine logs to see if any intruders are testing the perimeter.[2]

Some smaller businesses also implement these guidelines and best practices, too. However, a small business that is running on a shoestring budget is less likely to perform basic maintenance on their network infrastructure. The same way that a small business may not keep its own books or balance its checkbook—or maintain inventory well, or properly follow up with customers, or perform marketing activities—not all small businesses do everything well.

---

[2] Guidelines for agencies who wish to implement digital authentication can be found at: https://pages.nist.gov/800-63-3/sp800-63b.html.

Often times something like the network infrastructure—something that's hardly ever seen and very rarely thought about—gets installed as a set-and-forget service. That means the network switch that was installed three years ago may still have the default username and password, and the wireless network used by guests to check their personal email may also be on the same network where credit cards are processed. And it may be protected only by a weak username and password combination.

> *Your home computer is not like a crockpot. You can't just set-it-and-forget-it.*

Likewise, in the home, most people are thinking of ease-of-use rather than security when it comes to setting up a home network. Products come out of the box, they get plugged in, set up with an easy to use, minimal security tool like a Setup Wizard, defaults are left in place, people click "Next, Next, Next," and then everyone can get on the wi-fi network. That makes setup easy and user acceptance very high for all members of the family. But it provides almost no security and leaves vulnerable space in the family home.

Realistically, you may think you have nothing to hide, nothing of value sitting on your network. What difference does it really make? However, if you do any personal or business banking online, check stocks, pay bills, access credit cards, make online purchases, or share emails—or of course if you send racy texts or snapchats, and surf porn—all of this activity is exposed to those who have access to your home network. And frankly, if your home network was set up using default out-of-the-box settings, that grants access to anyone with the inclination to peruse your home network.

Also be aware that so-called "Smart Devices" may be susceptible to hacking. Smart TVs, smart speakers, Nest thermostats, refrigerators, and cameras should all be set up to routinely check for updates, or you may need to download and install these updates manually.

The Federal Bureau of Investigation recommends that you keep your IoT (Internet of Things) devices on a separate network from your primary devices such as laptops and cellphones. The Department of

Defense provides a list of best practices for keeping your home network secure available for download at:

https://dodcio.defense.gov/Portals/0/Documents/Cyber/Slicksheet_BestPracticesForKeepingYourHomeNetworkSecure_Web_update.pdf

War driving

You should also be aware that some hackers simply drive around neighborhoods checking to see what wireless connections are out there... noting which ones are available, and which ones can be logged into without a password or with only a simple password. There have been reports of "war driving groups" formed on Facebook where such information is then sold by region.

A number of reports exist from people who have purchased or done their own war drives, installing malware that "listens" for unprotected devices logging in to banking sites such as Chase.com, WellsFargo.com, and Citibank.com. When triggered, such hackers "screen scrape" or "keylog" information that gets sent unencrypted on the local network. They then "phone home" that data to the owner of the malware who then creates an amalgamation of 100, 1000, 10,000 of these records and then sells them on the dark web. When some folks with compromised accounts had these breaches investigated, it was discovered that there were sniffers on their local networks.

Whenever I go into a doctor's office or other professional office with a wi-fi network, I often try to access the office wireless network. While this is not technically war driving (I am walking into an office and waiting in a waiting room) it is similar in that I am testing for what is open and available to login to. I check to see if there's a way to get onto it, not to be malicious, but to determine whether the provider has protected the network, because it can speak volumes about other levels of security this office might have (or not have) in place. I once found that the hospital group that bought my doctor's office had installed a new Cisco network but never changed the root password from the default... until I mentioned it.

So again, let's assume that you do no banking online, you have no financial or personal info that you're worried about other people seeing online, and everything done is wholesome with nary a concern for what the neighbor or pastor/priest/rabbi/imam will think. A vulnerable network can also be used to launch spam or malware attacks next door or around the world by the practiced hacker. Some of the valuable assets on a home network are personal, private, financial, and medical info. There's also the computing power of idle machines that can be used for malicious purposes by organized and not-so-organized crime.

> *Even those with "nothing to hide" can be vulnerable if their computer or network is hijacked for malicious purposes against others.*

Botnets

A botnet is a group of computers assembled to use CPU cycles from the different machines to run malicious activities. This can be the encryption of target machines, anywhere in the world, where the attacker's identity and location can be hidden by storing information throughout this network. Hackers can also store the decryption keys for any machines that were encrypted. Botnets can also be used to send out spam or malware agents, recruiting agents for other botnets, or to perform denial-of-service attacks.

Many people have received an email from someone they know (or at least it looks like someone they know), yet they say, "Why would my friend send me this email?" only to later discover the "From" address is actually some other email address entirely.

Emails sent from a known and trusted person are more likely to be opened than discarded. If my computer were to become compromised, a piece of software may open my address book or contact list, and harvest that information. That data can then be sent back to a command server. This treasure of new email addresses may then be used to send a new malware email. This email will arrive with my name in the "From" display, however, when someone replies to it, they will (hopefully) discover the address is different than mine.

My contacts are likely to open an email that they think is from me, and if that email contains a malicious software payload, the cycle continues.

If this has happened to you, and you in turn write to your friend, "Hey, stop sending emails like this," it does no good. First, the real person wasn't the one who sent the spammy email, so he can do nothing about it. Second, maybe it wasn't even that friend's account that was originally hijacked. It might have been that his email address was simply listed on someone else's hacked address book.

How to tell the difference

First, check whether the "Sender" matches the "Reply To" address. Second, consider the content of the message. Is it spammy? Does it use fishy words or phrases? Does it contain a lot of spelling or grammar errors? (That may not be a deal-breaker for some of your friends.)

Hackers wear hats?

Hackers, in and of themselves, are not bad, but the word has come to mean something different than it did 30-40 years ago. Originally it just referred to someone who was trying to figure something out, sometimes using computers to determine the answer.

When cars were first invented, there were no mechanics. If you owned an automobile, you needed to be able to fix it yourself, because no other options existed. Gear heads would take pride in doing something others were not capable of doing for themselves. But today, many of us insert the key in the ignition, start the car, put it into drive, and press the gas and go. We do not know how to properly configure a fuel-injection system, or swap out the rear differential of our SUV. Nor do we want to know.

Similarly, tinkerers in garages and basements experimented with soldering resistors and wiring simple logic circuits together, creating a device that could perform addition and subtraction problems. These tinkerers became the first "hackers," hacking together solutions for problems when they couldn't go to a local hobby or computer store to buy a needed part.

In the early days of computing, when the world was transitioning from human computers (people who literally calculated every formula within a process) to machine computing, there was a constant push to reduce the amount of code it took to perform a task, because every action required time and energy. Speed and efficiency became highly relevant, for example, when NASA's human computers, ala *Hidden Figures* by Margot Lee Shetterly, needed to calculate the orbital re-entry so Neil Armstrong and his colleagues would not be flung out into deep space.

Today, "hackers" can be people who investigate systems and try to find vulnerabilities, or those who work to secure systems and processes. Hackers often probe to find backdoors and unreported weaknesses.

Why do people do this?
And what do they do with the information?

 A "whitehat" hacker may take this information and provide it to the company or vendor, looking to protect the world as a "greater good" service. Many times companies provide vulnerability bounties for those who report such exploits.

One problem is that these companies often pay poorly, if at all. Sometimes well-meaning hackers are told: "We're already addressing this bug," which makes some whitehats feel cheated for the time and energy they put in, and decide to release these vulnerabilities to the public if no timely changes emerge, even though the company claimed to be addressing the problem.

 This becomes the moment when whitehats turn to gray. A "grayhat" hacker feels the only way to get the potential vulnerability addressed is to make the public aware of it, thus forcing the company to fix the issue. If the grayhat chooses to accept money in exchange for this sensitive data, or if they are seen as violating laws, this can push the grayhat into the blackhat column.

A "blackhat" will work alone or with a group to find exploits and vulnerabilities, and then either use them themselves, or sell this information to other hackers (sometimes both) to leverage a payday.

The nuances between white, gray, and blackhat hackers are often lost during media soundbites, and a well-meaning whitehat can very quickly fall into the blackhat camp... especially when intellectual property rights are at stake.

Vulnerabilities exist in all kinds of products but are often easier to find on lower-end equipment. A cheap network switch purchased for under $50—as compared to $4500 for a higher-end product—has several differentiating factors including lower computing power, and fewer connections that can be made. The biggest factor, however, is the security of the device and the company's commitment to continue to patch vulnerabilities as they are identified. A small business might initially prefer the $50 switch because it was so inexpensive, but the choice may later end up being very costly.

Hackers may be motivated for different reasons. Some want fame, others enjoy a challenge, and of course money is a driving factor. More troubling, perhaps, is when processes designed to automate the exploit get distributed widely to "script kiddies." Wanna-be hackers can purchase such toolkits and launch an attack with no prior hacking knowledge, essentially like arsonists who set a building on fire just to watch it burn. They are motivated by peer recognition and boredom... and money. Since they have no specific target, it makes their actions (and the associated consequences) difficult to predict.

What motivates a hacker?

Fame
The Challenge
$$$$

Because the attacks are made so easy and are so random, the amount of data breached has increased exponentially. In 2019 alone, over 14 billion data records were *reported* lost or stolen. Less than 5% of that was encrypted data—meaning the information could be used without any additional effort. The rate of data loss is bound to increase.

Wanna cry?

In 2017, according to a government report, England's National Health Service (NHS) trusts were left vulnerable in a WannaCry Ransomware attack after cyber-security recommendations were not followed. At least 6,900 medical appointments were cancelled as a result, although NHS England said no patient data had been compromised or stolen.

These are the kinds of hackers I personally hate most because they bank on somebody else's work. They create a lot of havoc without understanding the ramifications of their actions.

Then there's organized crime, or perhaps we should call it disorganized crime. This includes criminal elements who exploit others as a business venture. They may employ their own developers in-house or purchase the methodology, but their goal is to take $1 and turn it into $10.

The 2019 CapitalOne data breach of 100 million customers was executed by an eccentric cybercriminal, Paige Thompson. However, she's quite the outlier. Most cybercriminals operate in highly organized groups based abroad. They approach their work like any business—except their revenue streams are stolen data and extortion.

An example of this is a group that cobbles together 100, 1000, even 10,000 machines to run a "Denial of Service" attack, bombarding a competitor's website so real customers can't access it. Alternatively, they may hold a competitor's content hostage, demanding a ransom payment.

Understanding the business model of hackers—and the value that a company's data represents to them—can be useful to help CFOs allocate appropriate resources to cyber defense. We may live in a time when first-world businesses rarely have to pay "protection money" to mafiosos, but hacking is the new organized crime, and these criminals are similarly ruthless about getting paid.

The value of your hacked PC

Modern cyberattacks—such as sophisticated phishing techniques utilizing phony emails that look quite real—can be profitable even with a seemingly low success rate around 1%. The cost of launching these attacks is low, and a single successful cyberattack can yield thousands or even millions of dollars in revenue.

The following pages contain a handy guide to help you understand why hackers might attempt to gain access to your personal and business computers for financial gain (see pages 76-77).

DANGERS OF A HACKED PC

Once your machine is taken over, it can be used for the following:

Web Server

- ⊗ Phishing Site
- ⊗ Malware Download Site
- ⊗ Warez/Piracy Server
- ⊗ Child Pornography Server
- ⊗ Spam Site

Email Attacks

- ⊗ Webmail Spam
- ⊗ Stranded Abroad Scams
- ⊗ Email Contact Harvesting
- ⊗ Associated Account Harvesting
- ⊗ Corporate Email Access

Virtual Goods

- ⊗ Online Gaming Characters
- ⊗ Online Gaming Goods
- ⊗ Cryptocurrency
- ⊗ PC Game License Keys
- ⊗ Operating System License Keys

Reputation Hijacking

- ⊗ Facebook
- ⊗ Twitter
- ⊗ LinkedIn
- ⊗ Instagram
- ⊗ TikTok

- ⊗ Spam Zombie
- ⊗ DDoS Extortion Zombie
- ⊗ Click Fraud Zombie
- ⊗ Anonymization Proxy
- ⊗ CAPTCHA Solving Zombie

Bot Activity

- ⊗ eBay/PayPal Fake Auctions
- ⊗ Online Gaming Fraud
- ⊗ Website FTP Credentials
- ⊗ Skype/VoIP Credentials
- ⊗ Client-Side Encryption Certificates

Account Credentials

- ⊗ Bank Account Data
- ⊗ Credit Card Data
- ⊗ Stock Trading Account
- ⊗ Mutual Fund / 401k Account

Financial Credentials

- ⊗ Hostage for Money Scam
- ⊗ Ransomware
- ⊗ Email Account Ransom
- ⊗ Webcam Extortion

Hostage Attacks

CHAPTER 6

A MATTER OF TRUST

In a previous chapter we talked about the Russian consulate and sensitive documents that were made vulnerable by copy repairmen. During service calls, a camera and recording device were embedded in photocopiers, allowing rival intelligence officials to have access to these confidential materials.

In the same vein, many corporations are in bed with the U.S. government. During the George W. Bush presidency, AT&T had a secret server farm where calls were monitored. Think *Enemy of the State*, when Gene Hackman's character talked about 18 acres of mainframe computers in Quantico, VA, dedicated to recording phone conversations. It's no secret the U.S. government is highly woven into the telecommunications industry. This is one of the reasons intelligence agencies discover how foreign governments use modern technology tools.[3]

Repair people

When you're aware of those who normally come in and out of your business and residence, you will be more likely to avoid potentially hazardous situations. If you have had the same meter reader for the last decade, but tomorrow a different meter reader shows up... on an unusual day... you will immediately be more hesitant to give them unbridled access to your property. It will send up a red flag, much like if you saw a foreign car or panel van parked on your street for days in a row.

---

[3] A *Slate* article highlights similar surveillance-related issues from a 2013 Senate investigation of Google.
https://slate.com/technology/2013/11/telcos-like-verizon-and-at-t-are-silent-on-nsa-surveillance.html

Access to homes is given up very easily to those who look authoritative. If you recall, an earlier chapter mentioned an episode of *Burn Notice* where the protagonist brags that he can get into almost any residence or office with a uniform and a clipboard... simply by carrying himself with authority. These are not just television and movie plots... such tactics are often used from a social engineering or data gathering perspective. In an attempt to plant a device to log keystrokes on computers or a hard drive on a photocopier or printer, a "repair person" may come onsite and ask the receptionist if anyone has called with a printer problem.

> *Don't be afraid or feel awkward about calling your service provider to confirm a repair person's identity.*

Again, if you're using a printer service company, and you've had the same repair people for a long time, seeing someone new should send up a red flag. Asking to see the repair person's credentials also may not solve the problem, because any social engineer who has done their homework will have created a false set of credentials to get into the space.

Don't be afraid or feel awkward about calling your service provider to confirm a repair person's identity.

Your vendors

The biggest breach from a retail sales perspective was the 2013 Target hack. Over 70 million individual credit card records were lost at the peak of holiday shopping season.

How that break-in took place: Target contracted with an HVAC supplier for all of its U.S. facilities. The HVAC supplier sub-contracted out some of the work because they didn't have locations in all the same cities, but to manage those installations, the products were all networked and monitored by the primary contractor.

This hack was the result of a multi-company failure. The HVAC computer networks were known (aka Target knew about them) and they were designed to be segregated and separate from all internal networks—including financial transactions—so the email systems, credit card services, and document management were supposed to be completely segregated from the HVAC monitoring systems.

However, at least *one* Target store had the two networks linked.

At some point, the HVAC company got hacked. It's still unclear if it was specifically "Target"ed, but this HVAC company was a known supplier for Target. Over the course of weeks and months, the group that infiltrated the HVAC company's system found a number of different exploits to put in place at the HVAC company itself.

Then the hackers found the real treasure trove—those networks that were cross-linked to the retail side of the Target house. What they did was the tech equivalent of sticking a coffee cup under a running faucet, and started scooping up the data as it went by.

Over the course of about half a year, they netted more than 70 million credit card records. Reputationally, Target is still suffering to this day.

The 2014 Sony hack has some similarities. People paid big money for high-end Sony gaming systems. Their credit card data was kept on file to make in-app purchases simple and instantaneous. This was before the Sony hack you may have heard about that involved the Seth Rogen movie and North Korea, but was far more invasive.

What types of devices?

There are examples of hard drives on photocopiers and printers, listening devices in conference rooms or C-level executive offices or those of their assistants, and keyloggers that send info back to a centralized server to extract sensitive or proprietary data. There are even executives of the U.S. Chamber of Commerce who had their thermostats bugged with a network listening device. The device was only discovered after documents were printed on several U.S. Chamber's printers—in Chinese. This was a lobbying office in Washington, D.C., where strategy decisions were being made on how to lobby the government to exclude foreign businesses and promote U.S.-based business to our elected leaders.[4]

---

[4] www.wsj.com/articles/SB10001424052970204058404577110541568535300

While these are extreme examples, it only takes one device connected to a network to compromise an entire company's data. One of the easiest ways of infiltrating a company's network is to install malware on a handful of USB drives and scatter them in an employee parking lot of a targeted company or agency. Nearly half the people who find such a device will pick it up and plug it into their computers in the office.[5] If the company or agency's logo is on the device, that number spikes to 66%. In many cases the employee is simply trying to discern who has accidentally lost the device so they may return it.

Often we think social engineering plays on others' stupidity. This is a very cynical view. Most social engineering plays on people's altruism and societal norms. In our culture (not so much in New York, but in other places), if someone says "Good morning" to you, the proper response is "Good morning." It's an automatic reaction.

When people start engaging casually with one another, these programmed responses bypass many of our filters. Once that protective layer is breached, a certain percentage of individuals will accept the conversation that follows. That's why social engineering works.

Half the time when someone picks up a wallet, they open it—not to steal the money, but to see who it belongs to, so they can return it. Likewise, if I dropped something in a parking lot where my colleagues worked, I would hope they would pick it up and return it to me.

The only way to open a "lost" USB drive is to plug it into something. And no matter how often people are told, "Don't plug things into your computer," it happens all the time.

They should've known better

At a 2017 technology conference filled with over 1500 seasoned IT security professionals, scantily-clad women were stationed at the entrance to the main hall, giving away USB drives with a new company's logo.

Not everybody who entered the venue took the drive, but of those who did, over 30% immediately plugged them into their laptops.

[5] https://www.theregister.com/2016/04/11/half_plug_in_found_drives/

Meanwhile the speaker on stage clicked through his presentation and then announced, "These are your fellow conference goers who have plugged in the USB drive that we just gave out, even though we tell our customers never to plug in drives when you don't know their origin."

Then he advanced the slide and a chart populated with machine names of people who had opened the drive and were connected to wi-fi.

Intellectually, these people knew better, but social engineering drove their behavior. Actually there were several social engineering cues at work here:

- If it's free, it's for me.
- If a beautiful woman offers you something, accept it.
- If I'm at an event that I (or my company) paid money to attend, it's a safe space, so nothing bad can happen to me here.
- Free wi-fi? I'm connecting.
- New company? I've gotta plug this in to find out what they're offering.

This is social engineering at its best, leveraging multiple cues to prompt a desired behavior.

Hidden devices in common spaces

When strangers have access to common areas in your office or home, it can create other problems. There are many documented cases of people of questionable character installing video cameras in ladies restrooms and personal home bathrooms, either recording or streaming video content to paid subscribers. It may not be your cup of tea, but someone is paying for it.

Instances of the same kind of privacy breaches have occurred in hotels and Airbnb-style short-term rental properties. A 2019 *Huffington Post* article outlines the Barker family's European vacation with their five children, when they discovered a hidden camera in the smoke alarm.

Next time you are traveling, you should automatically assume that you're being watched. A well-hidden device will be challenging to spot. You can begin by scanning the wi-fi network for devices. Within the property, you can also look for things that are out of place. Mirrored surfaces may disguise a hidden camera. But the reality is, if someone is good at hiding cameras, you are probably not going to find them.

School devices

Safe spaces such as schools and aftercare centers shouldn't be places where parents or children need to be worried about falling easy prey. A quick scan of today's news, however, tells a much different story.

The equivalent of nanny-cams in daycare or afterschool facilities where working parents can look in on their children offers opportunities for voyeurs and other miscreants to use borrowed or stolen credentials to spy on children, unbeknownst to parents or facility administrators.

In pre-pandemic times, there were concerns about school-provided laptops/Chromebooks/iPads, where teachers were not properly vetted (or whose backgrounds were questionable) have turned video cameras on to spy on students while they were at home doing homework or using their devices in the evening. Video captured from these sessions could be sold on websites, or just viewed voyeuristically for thrills. Today, with more education happening online, these devices are almost always turned on, and to ensure student engagement, administration often requires students' cameras to be on as well. This is yet another potential vulnerability where individuals with access to login credentials now have a treasure trove of viewing choices.

So how do we protect ourselves? The simple answer is the best. When the machine is not in use, place a sticky note or other covering over the camera. Make sure the device is powered off and stored, rather than facing into a child's bedroom or living room.

It's very easy to get a Zoom password to join/watch a classroom of thirty kids. A teacher who is responsible for thirty students can only scan attendees periodically while also teaching the lesson content. Most interlopers will not linger long, but if they do, they will be found.

WEBCAM PRIVACY:
When not in use, cover the camera, or power off the device.

An appropriate Zoom setting can vary widely depending on the rules of the school, the mores of the community, and even the politics of the time. However, a good rule of thumb is: The view presented by the student should really be a headshot only, from the neck up, not a full view of bedroom space that might contain posters or items of questionable content. Predators who have detailed information about a personal setting may be able to use it more effectively to harass or bully children.

Ultimately it is the parents' responsibility to make sure children are aware of the dangers and what these things could potentially mean to their reputation or future selves. In the case of children who are too young to make these decisions, obviously it falls to the parents to act in a way that protects the child's best interests.

IT and travel

All you really need to do is look at Rudy Giuliani and his prevalence of butt-dialing reporters, while in the middle of doing things he shouldn't be doing, to understand that any device with a microphone can pick up sound and broadcast it.

> "Just make sure that all meetings take place at the Four Seasons. It needs to be between the crematorium and the sex shop, because that's the only places I want to be."[6]

---

[6] For the story on Trump's press conference-gone-wrong and fumbles by his attorney, Rudy Giuliani, visit https://www.esquiremag.ph/politics/news/how-american-fascism-died-between-a-sex-shop-and-a-crematorium-a2416-20201112

Similar to the vulnerabilities of laptop use at home, you have to know what wi-fi network you are connected to. Whether it's on an airplane, in a coffee shop, or in your hotel room, the wi-fi network that's listed may be innocuous or it could be rife with pitfalls.

A common hacking technique is to set up a network repeater in a shop at an airport gate, a hotel room, or even a busy conference. Unsuspecting people connect their laptops or cell phones to that free wi-fi. Malware and other nefarious software can be installed on their machines, controlled by someone else, and data can be captured even before a VPN connection can be made.

At the Sochi Olympics, it was found that pretty much any device turned on at the Olympic Village came home with malware and infections. In fact, when traveling to China, many routinely use burner devices, planning to either throw them away or remove and replace the hard drive after returning from their trip.

Delivery people

Google's Nest Hello and Amazon's Ring Doorbell are video doorbell cameras that allow you to keep a watchful eye on your property. Under normal circumstances, such devices can ping you when a package is delivered or someone steps within an allotted distance. They can also include a variety of features like facial recognition and voice control, though they may be affected by outdoor lighting conditions.

Why is Ring Doorbell so popular these days? It's because people in rural areas and some suburban areas have had material stolen off their front porch or out of their driveway. Sometimes the theft is committed by an individual just going around the neighborhood, but it also gets perpetrated by someone posing as a delivery person.

If you know "Fred" is your regular delivery person, when someone besides Fred shows up, especially if it happens at a non-routine delivery time, that should spark concern. This may be different now that companies like Amazon contract deliveries outside of USPS, UPS, and FedEx, but it's still important to recognized your regular mailman as well as the FedEx and UPS deliverymen.

As we order from delivery services like Uber Eats and Door Dash and Grub hub, we're giving outsiders even more access to our personal and office space.

In many areas of life, we have a false sense of security. We like to fool ourselves into believing that every delivery person or Lyft driver has been properly vetted. At the same time, we also swing wildly in the other direction and assume that we can provide security at a fraction of the cost compared to professional installation and monitoring services. This is one of the reasons we see an increase in the installation of "smart devices" and alarm systems. This helps us to fall back on that false sense of security. You still need to know who's coming or going.

A common technique when preparing to rob an unoccupied house is to pose as a food delivery person. Ring the doorbell, and if someone answers, confirm the (wrong) delivery address. "I've got this anchovy pizza for 23 Chestnut Lane..." when in actuality the home is on Chestnut Road.

Ultimately you will need to balance your safety and security and remain aware of your surroundings. Don't make yourself too crazy about it.

CHAPTER 7

PASSWORD MANAGEMENT

In this day and age there are way too many passwords needed to navigate day-to-day logins to your various accounts. As a home user, it makes sense to have just *one* place to store your passwords and know they are under lock and key. If you are a business owner, however, password management is even more critical.

So why should we care about passwords and password management? Because password security is perhaps the biggest threat to an organization or family's online and financial security. That may sound extreme, but if you consider that stolen and weak passwords are responsible for over 80% of all security breaches, we really need to figure out how to alleviate this vulnerability.

In 2015, the Office of Personnel Management was breached at the federal level, making the personnel data of 21.5 million current and former employees vulnerable. This was not just names or addresses, but also Social Security numbers, drivers licenses, and in some cases, password information. The background check details of 19.7 million individuals was breached, along with data related to 1.8 million non-applicant spouses or cohabitants, and 5.6 million fingerprint records.

When a database is hacked, its rows and columns of information can be hijacked into a sort of spreadsheet. But a database's information is often stored in several different layers. One level might contain only a name and an identification number—something known as a "key record." Other levels of spreadsheet-style data will be connected only by this ID number or key record tag. Without that topmost layer, it would be difficult to know what Social Security number is connected with which person in the database. We call this a "relational database." The key record is literally the key that unlocks the treasure of the database's information.

What made the Office of Personnel Management's breach so significant is that these "key records" were obtained... and for employees of the federal government, background checks are extensive, so this database contained massive records of each employee's life, replete with information they were required to submit in order to be issued security clearances. Beyond names, addresses, telephone numbers and personal Social Security numbers, it also included things like spouses' names, children's names, and parents' names, dates and places of birth... as well as every address at which the employee had ever lived.

> *Password security is perhaps the biggest threat to an organization or family's online and financial safety.*

Because many websites and financial institutions offer alternate ways for you to access your account through "security questions," when armed with info like your mother's maiden name, the hackers could leverage the stolen data to reset account passwords for every email address ever used, which would in turn allow them to confirm password changes on other sites like American Express, Wells Fargo, the Small Business Administration, and even student loans.

During a password reset, most sites ask for a username and current password, and give multiple attempts to get the password correct. In the event that doesn't work, the hackers could try the Forgot-My-Password feature, answering security questions like place of birth, or previous street address, then confirm it from the already hacked email address associated with the account.

To round out this line of attack, when a database holding sensitive information like usernames, passwords, current address, mother's maiden name, and date of birth is paired with a list of all your previous addresses and spousal information, the hacker is no longer stymied by a security question like "What street did you live on in the 3rd grade?"

How to protect yourself

So what does a password management system do to protect you from this? Many people use very simple passwords, in fact, the most commonly used one in 2019 and 2020 was "password."

People often use the same password for their banking app, mortgage app, and even their children's remote-learning platform... so it will be easier to remember, rather than wasting time and becoming frustrated. A password management system allows you to remember the "one password to rule them all" while still maintaining highly secure passwords that are unique to each site.

If we start with the belief that every website and application should have its own unique and complex password, the question that naturally follows is "How the hell do I remember them all?" Short of writing passwords on a sticky note and putting them under your keyboard—which is done more than you'd like to believe—there is another way. Using more complex passwords of 10, 15, even 20 characters with a mix of uppercase, lowercase, and alpha-numerics becomes much easier when stored in a password management system. You then only need to remember one master password to gain access to all the others.

Today we have more websites, sometimes tens and even hundreds that we may use once a month, once a quarter, once a year, or once every five years. For example, I created a password to sign up for my daughter's student loan, then four years later when I had to sign up for my son's student loan, I had no idea what that earlier password was. I had only used it once.

When using a password management tool, that system doesn't care how complex each password is... whether it's five characters or 50. We only have to worry about remembering the master password and setting the rules of complexity for any passwords stored in the system. You can even use a pass-phrase which may be a common line of dialogue bantered about between you and your spouse, as long as it meets the rules you've established.

Even if your vital key record information is compromised, this additional step makes it less likely that your various accounts can be hacked.

Sometimes it's okay to lie

You can also protect yourself by adapting your responses when setting up security questions/answers. For example, rather than using your mother's real maiden name, you could use your mother-in-law's maiden name. For me though, I go even further and use a completely fictitious name. But I don't have to remember what it is, because I have it stored in my password management system.

Likewise, you don't have to use the real city of your birth, or the city where your parents met, or the year you actually graduated high school. Instead, use the password management tool to save not only your various complex and secure passwords, but also the specific answers used for security questions.

Again, even if your key records get compromised in a massive data leak at a state or national level, right down to the most intimate details... if your answers to security questions were fictitious, it is an added level of obfuscation and makes it more difficult to have your passwords reset without your knowledge or consent.

What else can a password management system do?

Another feature of a password management tool is the ability to change a large number of passwords quickly. As a business owner, for example, if someone leaves or is fired from your company, you can change all the passwords that person had access to within your business. From an audit standpoint, you can access forensic information to learn who logged in using what password and when. Even if you use a shared password amongst a dozen people in your company, you can track usage at the individual level. You can also scan the dark web to see if those passwords are in use, and to what extent.

But wait, there's more! A password management system can be configured to perform specific actions in advance of certain life events. For example, the system can be designed to detect whether you have not logged in within a certain number of days. In such a case, you can designate that your passwords, or some of them, will be released to a trusted individual. This can be vital in the event that you fall ill or are hurt, when access to certain passwords may be required. For example, a business partner may need to run payroll for your employees, or your lawyer, spouse, or caregiver could need access to critical lifesaving information.

A well-designed and utilized password management system is the equivalent of a medic-alert bracelet for your business.

In the digital age, this is the equivalent of having a note taped to your refrigerator with important medical data that an EMT might need if the ambulance were called to your house... like a medic-alert bracelet for your business.

Use it or lose it

However, no matter how great a password management tool is, if it is difficult to use, you're not going to adopt it!

Various web browsers—Microsoft Edge, Firefox, Chrome, and their applications for Android and iPhone—offer easy plugins to remember your passwords, but in the event of data loss or hardware malfunction, without a comprehensive backup of that plugin's content, your passwords are lost to the ether. Even worse, they're stored with little to no encryption and easily retrievable from your hardware. Even worse than that, when you sync your Chrome or Edge profile across multiple devices, you're now storing critical information, unencrypted, in many places. This increases the likelihood that your passwords could become compromised.

Using a password management system, however, allows you access to all your information, without worry of potentially losing it or having it stolen, as long as you can remember your master password.

Password Boss

Password Boss is a password management tool that stores encrypted credentials on a cloud-based service where you retain the key to unlock the system. It has plugins that can be used on multiple operating system platforms and all major web browsers that doesn't compromise its security for ease of use.

One of the key features that sold me on the product was the ability to create an offline master password that can be used to unencrypt the data. Why is this so important? Password Boss, as a company, will not retain a master key to your encrypted data, which is what makes it secure and a preferred solution. Only you have access to your stuff.

I feel so strongly about this product, I've struck a special arrangement with Password Boss to offer readers of this book a free month's trial.

Go to
https://keepmesafe.club/password
to claim your gift now.

Please, please, please...

Whatever you do, do not write your master password down on a sticky note and put it on your monitor!

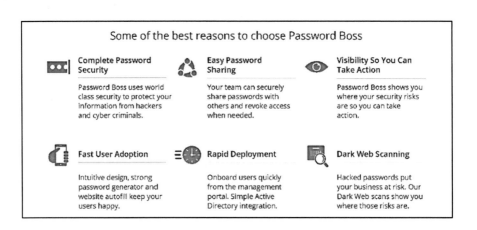

Some of the best reasons to choose Password Boss

Complete Password Security
Password Boss uses world class security to protect your information from hackers and cyber criminals.

Easy Password Sharing
Your team can securely share passwords with others and revoke access when needed.

Visibility So You Can Take Action
Password Boss shows you where your security risks are so you can take action.

Fast User Adoption
Intuitive design, strong password generator and website autofill keep your users happy.

Rapid Deployment
Onboard users quickly from the management portal. Simple Active Directory integration.

Dark Web Scanning
Hacked passwords put your business at risk. Our Dark Web scans show you where those risks are.

CHAPTER 8

BACKUPS

Throughout the book, we've made the argument that the best way to protect yourself from different potential threats is through education and planning. The reality is that no matter how well you plan, the more you learn about the threats in the cyber world, the more you come to realize that having other options is critical. When it comes to your files—either personally or for business—a good backup plan goes a long way.

When a new virus or ransomware or malware is released or a data breach occurs, one of the first questions people want answered is: "Is my data safe?" This question has meaning on several different levels. On the most basic level, the question asks "Does anyone else have access to this information—financial records, photos, corporate records, or intellectual property that I hold dear?"

On another level is the question of data integrity. Although losing snapshots of your children in their early years would be devastating, when viewing a photo of your child, you could easily confirm that the photo is indeed of your children. So long as the picture is present and you can look at it, you have a high degree of confidence that the file is in good working order. But a quick review may not be sufficient to confirm the integrity of other kinds of data. When looking at business files, you want to be assured the proposal you're about to send your customer is the correct final version. Even with incorrect figures and missing data, you may win the business with your proposal, but at what cost? The deal may get done with information that's missing or under terms you can't carry. You might even have to do the work without making any profit. Maybe worse, files that are unreadable may have been altered and contain malware or viruses that spread to a client and beyond.

Whether files are damaged, encrypted, or just incorrect, a working, valid, tested backup provides added peace of mind that your data is true and accurate.

Now let's define some terms you need to be familiar with when discussing data backup.

RPO

Recovery Point Objective is the point in time that data is being recovered from. This is a specific point in time, or a recovery from a specific distance in time behind the data loss. Your backup strategy should have a defined RPO that meets your business needs.

As an example, most small businesses have an RPO of one business day. That means if it is Thursday at 5:30 P.M., and for some reason all data is lost from a workstation or data storage, the recovery point objective is Wednesday at 5:30 P.M. If the most data you can afford to lose is 15 minutes, then your RPO needs to be 15 minutes in the past from the point of data loss. That means 15 minutes from when the data loss started... not when it was discovered!

RPO – Recovery Point Objective

The point in time where the last data changes were made and will be recovered to.

Another way to look at this is, if you were a doctor and had no paper files and everything was done on your computer, and 20 patients were seen in one day, could you afford to lose all the chart updates, notes from patient visits, and prescription info, for one full day? Would this be a violation of state medical records retention?

If you were an accountant in the middle of tax season and lost all the tax documents you were preparing for one day's worth of clients, would that be a position you could easily recover from, or would it be a catastrophic event for your business?

RTO

Recovery Time Objective means that whatever time it takes to get to your predetermined recovery point objective (RPO), it must take place within a predetermined time objective (RTO). For example, if your RPO is one business day and it takes seven hours to recover all of your data back to a point of 24 hours before the loss event occurred, that seven hours would be your RTO.

Why is this important? When personal and commercial vendors sell solutions for backup, they very often speak about backing up *all* of your data and being able to recover *all* of your data. The "all of your data" needs to be in quotes... because who determines what "all of your data" includes?

If you're a sole proprietor with one computer, using a product like Carbonite, the amount of time it takes to back up the files on your computer is limited by the speed of your machine, the speed of your internet connection, and is dependent on both of those things being up and running. How that software is configured will determine how quickly the initial backup (or "seed") will occur.

RTO – Recovery Time Objective

The amount of time it takes to restore your data from backup.

In the event you've signed up for a backup solution, and you're backing up all the data on your computer, without excluding unnecessary files (like the operating system files that would not be required if you completely replaced the computer), and you have a 512GB hard drive and a 100mbps internet connection, it could take several weeks for the initial seed to occur. If you lost data between the time you started, but before the initial seed completes, you would not be able to recover a single thing.

So the reason RTO is an important factor in building a backup solution is that if your RPO is 24 hours and the RTO is 8 hours, effectively no business can be done with new data or access to the files on the computer or server for 8 hours while the restore is taking place. Are orders being entered on paper and need to be keyed in when the systems come back online? Is the business running a Point of Sale system and nothing can be rung up until the server is restored and up and running? Were you in the middle of a big project and you need to get to the files on your computer or server? That can't be done during a restore. When considering backup, it's not only how long it takes to complete a backup, but how long it takes to restore the data that is critical.

Full backup vs. differential

When considering a backup solution, the type of backup—full or differential—is another decision point. In a full backup, all data you selected for backup (even the data that hasn't changed in two years) will be backed up. This means if a full backup is done daily, there's a huge amount of redundant data being read and written. This will consume a large amount of space and use more resources, including time, and cost more for storage. When backing up using a differential process, a starting point collects all the data and then subsequent processes only capture files that have been changed.

While more cost-effective, both in time and storage, a restore from a differential can be problematic. If an initial full backup is then built up with six months of differential tasks, a restore will need to go to the original full backup and then build through each of the subsequent daily differentials over that same period of time. This can greatly increase the amount of time it takes to restore data. Additionally, if even one differential backup is damaged, nothing past that damaged process will be restorable.

Technologies that use an initial seed backup plus differentials, then create a break-point where a new base of all changes are rolled together, creating a fail-safe. By doing this, it allows for a speedier recovery as you do not have to restore all the backups from the first seed down to the last differential backup. Instead you can start from the last full backup and apply the recent differentials. As a word of caution, only by having tested the full backup and differentials will you be certain your data is viable.

Finally, it's not only about getting the data out; it's about what it takes to get your data back. Remember, there are multiple factors that limit the time it takes to restore your data. When using an offsite backup process, the speed of your internet connection, the restore prioritization you've purchased, and the backup company's bandwidth allocated to restores all come into play. Do you have another device to restore your data to if you have lost your laptop (in the cab, on an airplane, dropped from a height)? In that case, getting the data back may not be enough. You still need to have a replacement laptop or another computer to restore the data to.

Assuming all of these factors are in place and known, the fine print of most offsite backup solutions state that it can take three times as long to restore your data as it took to back it up in the first place. If you had a complete system loss and you had to restore x amount of data in y amount of time, does your backup solution meet the requirements that you've set out in terms of a recovery timeframe?

Now, RTO and RPO are factors in business backups, however in most personal backups, as long as we know the data is recoverable, we're less concerned about how long it takes. Knowing that your child's baby pictures are safe and can be recovered may be enough. The likelihood you'll need them immediately is low. However, data fidelity is a concern for everyone.

What is data fidelity?

Anyone who's ever downloaded a file for work or pleasure and opened that file only to get a "This file cannot be read" message, or "This file is corrupted," or even though the file is named correctly, it doesn't contain the information you expected will have felt the frustration of data fidelity.

The time to test your backup files is not after you've had a catastrophic data loss.

The concept of data fidelity is that the data you are looking for will be there in a good and usable format when you need it. Whether this is family pictures, scanned images of family trees, or past medical or financial records, business plans, contracts with customers, customer data, or intellectual property, there's nothing worse than thinking you have a good backup, only to realize when you need it, that you do not.

There are entire departments in Fortune 500 companies dedicated exclusively to performing backups and doing regular random tests of them to ensure recoverability within the required timeframe, with data fidelity checks as a final critical step.

Another concern regarding data fidelity is whether the data will be restorable using the technology available at the time it's required. About 20 years ago, a company called IOGEAR made little blue zip drives. You could store 100MB, which was considered a lot at the time, and you could go into most office supply shops (Staples, Office Depot, Office Max) and buy both a reader and the discs. A lot of people chose to back up their most important files in this format. IOGEAR then went to gigabytes of data and hundreds of gigabytes of data. None of the drives were backwards compatible. Today if you try to buy an IOGEAR product to read your zip drives you may have a very hard time finding one.

Why does this matter?

If you backed up important company files that haven't been used in 10 years and you need to retrieve them, you have to make sure that:

- the necessary hardware still exists
- the hardware is compatible with the current OS running on your computer
- the media was stored properly and is actually accessible

What happens if your family photos passed to you by a now deceased loved one were all transferred onto these discs? Same problem.

In the original *Men in Black,* Tommy Lee Jones's character brings up this concept while showing Will Smith's character an even smaller compact disc, asking "Do you know what this means? It means I have to buy the W*hite* album again." It's a funny problem to have, but if you know anyone who invested in laser discs for their favorite movies, they're either a specific type of audiophile, or they've bought the movie again on DVD or Blu-ray or 4K or maybe all formats... only to now watch it on Netflix, Amazon Prime, or some other streaming service.

What is ubiquitous today may be rare tomorrow. Again, those Fortune 500 companies have, within their backup staff, people who retain old tape drive systems, sometimes four, five or six versions back, because their regulatory obligation requires them to be able to access information up to ten years old. If a deal or contract is still active, they may have to go back even further.

It costs a great deal of money to maintain those systems and make them able to work with newer technology. For example, backup systems that worked great with Windows 3.1.1 don't have natural interfaces to work with Windows 10.

Choosing what to backup wisely

As you just learned above, it may cost a lot of time and money to convert from one backup methodology to another, and since it also costs time and money to backup or restore data, you want to be very aware of what it is you choose to back up.

When a sole proprietor or an individual backs up data from a computer at home, the question of what needs to be backed up should be taken into consideration. Does the operating system (Windows 10, Mac Catalina) need to be backed up? Probably not. All the Word docs, Excel docs, photos in jpg, png, tif, pdf format? Probably yes. What about specific configuration files? If you've saved your passwords to your computer, and that file is in a specific location within the operating system, you may need to back up that specific file, dependent on what software you're using.

It will save you a lot of time and money to only back up the things you need versus backing up everything.

When we set up backups, we should think about the time it takes to do the setup, and to dig into the nitty gritty of where files live. This can be onerous. However, now is when you have the most time. The best time to determine what files you need is *not* in the middle of an emergency.

If you've chosen the default settings, backed up your entire C Drive, and your restore time is seven days, and meanwhile you need the Last Will and Testament for someone who's just passed away, or to find your client data because a computer just died, you'll be in a much bigger rush to restore that data immediately and it will be far more difficult to do so.

Today when you subscribe to a music service and you upload the files you're interested in, for access to Apple's iTunes store, it's unlikely your Britney Spears album will be uploaded. However, your Grateful Dead bootleg of their San Diego 3rd night tour in 1983, second encore is probably going to be uploaded. The algorithms that give you access to data on iTunes knows that you've purchased a copy of a common album when it's Britney and there's no reason to re-upload the data since it's probably the same as 100,000 others. However, the other very specific music may exist nowhere else.

Focus your music and photo backups on files that are unique and irretrievable.

This example is how we should view the music we choose to back up. In today's world, very few people actually have all of their music downloaded to the computer. Even when you buy music from iTunes, you're given access to that data from whatever device is signed in with your ID. So, will you really need to back up data that's available on any device you can log onto to hear? Probably not. Why spend your precious backup time—and more importantly, restore time—on files that are available pretty much anywhere?

You want to focus on files that are unique and irretrievable, except through your backup. Likewise, if you've purchased a thousand stock images from Adobe, you don't need to back those up. If you've modified any images, or have original images only you possess, you'd want to back up these unique products.

Online services

MS One Drive, Google Drive, Apple Drive... read the fine print. Who is responsible for your data? How many versions are they responsible to retain? How long are the backups kept?

The fine print on GSuite say that they're not responsible for the data unless you pay them an additional fee. GSuite, Apple, and Microsoft generally store backups for 30 days. Therefore, if you've changed a file or deleted a file, in both cases your original file will be available on backup for 30 days. On the 31st day, that file will be purged from the system unless you have additional backup retention in place (and are paying for it). Therefore, you may lose data you thought you had.

For example, let's say you hired a summer intern. In early June they're just getting the hang of how to use your company's programs and filing systems. In the first week or two, while trying to clean up some folders, a bunch of files are deleted. If you have the standard system in place from GSuite, Apple, or MS, come mid-July, all those deleted files will be irretrievable.

It's important to note all of these cloud services, as well as most others, interface with some type of backup solution where you can control the retention and retrieval levels of any files deleted or purged.

Final word

The cost of digital storage today is a fraction of what it was five years ago, which is a fraction of what it was five years before that. Data prices are regularly dropping, and the ability to store the data is going up. It's still important to decide what it is you want to store, and the likelihood of ever using it, to really determine what solution is best for you.

I'm a big stickler about this because I visit sites where a sole proprietor puts a solution on their computer and backs up everything, but three-quarters of the content is taken up by the operating system and old versions of software like MS Office and Adobe Acrobat... when all that stuff can be reinstalled and does not need to be backed up. It slows down the backup time and makes it less likely you will truly be able to back up the important items you care about most. More importantly, it slows the restore time, which is where the real problem comes into focus.

You're always making a choice between backup time and backup cycle time. If you need backups available to the latest fifteen minutes, then you risk having incomplete backup files if the cycle time isn't completed within fifteen minutes. These backup systems do exist. They are not usually found in small business environments because most small businesses believe they are cost prohibitive. They are not when the right tool is used.

Go to
https://keepmesafe.club/backups
to claim your gift now.

There are a number of criteria I recommend when designing a backup solution.

The first consideration is the speed to restore local data from a server or servers and local workstations in an office. Your data should be readily available to retrieve as a single file or folder with a number of files inside or in a database.

The second consideration is that the data should also be transported and stored offsite periodically to ensure that if the physical location is compromised through theft, fire, or water damage that data can still be retrieved.

Your third consideration should be that the data transfer offsite should be automatic, removing the need for human intervention—no storing a USB drive in a local bank vault.

A fourth consideration is that the offsite storage should meet the requirements of the regulations of your industry, at a minimum, and when possible, far exceed those basic levels.

Next, the system and service should be able to back up cloud-based instances of email, data stores, and even virtual servers.

A sixth consideration is the ability to virtualize the environment, bringing up an entire working environment remotely in the event that the space is inaccessible or ceases to exist.

Finally, the seventh consideration is the ability to restore to brand new hardware in the event that gear has to be completely replaced due to a total site loss (from theft, fire, or water damage).

To recap, things to consider in your backup solution should include:

1. Speed of restoration
2. Offsite data storage
3. Automation of offsite data storage
4. Meet or exceed industry standards for offsite data storage
5. Cloud-based backup of emails, data stores, and virtual servers
6. Ability to virtualize a computing environment to work remotely if needed
7. Ability to restore to brand new hardware

We recommend a solution to our clients that meets these needs and is flexible enough to start with a single-person business and scale up to thousands of employees across multiple sites and locations. Proper planning and designing for growth are important to be able to reuse materials in place. However, beginning with a system that can meet your needs from the start is affordable and within reach.

Go to
https://keepmesafe.club/backups
and take your next step toward a system
that will keep your business and family safe.

CHAPTER 9

FUTURE THREATS &

THE IOT (INTERNET OF THINGS)

Today, many people recognize the phrase "IP address" but not everyone knows what an IP Address is or what it does. At its simplest, the definition of an IP address is a numeric value assigned to a resource on the public internet. While that is a valid definition, it really doesn't answer the "WHY" question and hardly answers the "WHAT."

Let's attack this from a different direction. The problem that an IP address looks to solve is how to *find* a specific resource you're looking for in a diverse, dispersed, worldwide computer network. By "find," I don't mean how you pick it out of a haystack like using a search engine to find the perfect recipe for sourdough bread. I mean how will your web browser on your computer or cell phone navigate to where the resource is located to bring up the pictures and text you are searching for?

If you're in Galveston, Texas, sitting at your home computer, looking to find the perfect sourdough recipe, and you know it's on AllRecipes.com, you may not have any idea if the server that's hosting that website is in New York or California or even in the United States. If it happens to be in California, is it located in San Diego or Sacramento?

As mentioned, an IP address is a unique identifier that helps your computer locate data, devices, and websites. If you think of the internet like the U.S. Postal Service, a five-digit ZIP code will give a fairly specific location for an address. In Las Vegas, for example, the MGM Hotel has its own ZIP code, but in Wyoming one ZIP code can cover an awful lot of ground. The ZIP+4 system provides even greater precision, sometimes down to a specific post office box.

On the internet, when you want to find a specific website, even though you type in "AllRecipes.com," your internet web browser, through a series of protocols, must then look up that URL to determine its specific IP address.

Now all of this is interesting, but it's only the appetizer. *Warning: extra geeky...*

Some people are familiar with the term "IPv4," where "IP" stands for Internet Protocol, the "v" is version, and "4" indicates the fourth version of the protocol. More people will recognize that 192.168.1.1 looks like something needed for their computer to get onto the internet.

The four sections of numbers, separated by periods, are called octets. The reason each grouping is called an octet is because the numbers 0–255 are represented by eight places on the binary coding system. In theory, each octet can house any number between 0 and 255. This would mean the scope of available IP addresses in IPv4 ranges from 0.0.0.0 through 255.255.255.255.

This is not 100% accurate because there are ranges of reserved IP ranges for internal private networks. They usually start with 10., 172., and 192. [Additionally, there is something called "broadcast traffic" which usually uses .255 in the final octet, but if you're already at that level of geekiness, call me about a job.]

So, based on the way IPv4 is created, after subtracting about 18 million addresses that are reserved for internal, non-routable traffic, it has 4,296,967,296 usable, internet-facing IPs.

When looking up "AllRecipes.com," there is a single IP address that either matches directly to that URL or matches up to a server where that URL is being hosted... along with possibly hundreds of other websites... and it's up to the server to present the correct website when queried.

When IPv4 was first deployed for production in the ARPANET in 1983, it was widely viewed that having over four billion external-facing IP addresses would be more than enough for hundreds of years. In fact it worked well enough for forty years.

However, when the fourth iteration of the IP protocol was first deployed, there was no concept of having a networked thermostat or wi-fi connected light switch in every household. Or if these were considered, certainly a networked toaster or refrigerator was never part of the equation.

The "Internet of Things" (IoT) assumes that people want to have everything network-accessible. (Perhaps more likely, the IoT assumes that *retailers* want to sell every product that they make as network-accessible.) Arguments can be made that many people don't desire this, or that having every device and appliance network-accessible is not even a good idea. But those are philosophical or religious arguments outside the scope of this book. The Internet of Things *is* coming, and whether it should or should not exist, you should be aware of its ramifications.

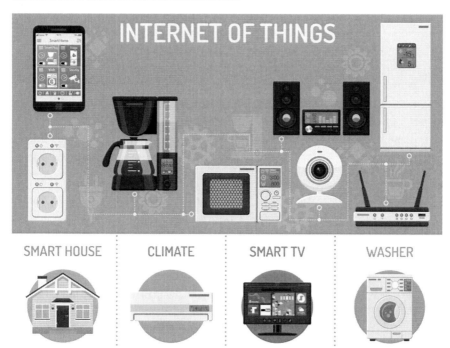

An IPv4 is a 32-bit address (four sets of eight binary digits, 4 x 8 =32 bits). The newer protocol, IPv6, provides 128-bit addresses. This means there are 2^{128} addresses available. From a visual perspective, if the more than four-billion IPv4 addresses filled the surface area of a golf ball, then the IPv6 addresses would equal the surface area of the sun.

With network-accessible appliances, as with most things in life, we haven't asked *should* we do something, but rather *can* we do it. While an advertisement during the Superbowl 2020 showed an idyllic image where people traveling in their car remotely turned up the heat in their home, started a fire in the gas fireplace, set mood lighting, and played a romantic sonata prior to the couple's arrival at their winter getaway... there are some serious downsides.

When the IoT fully comes online, there will be good things made available and the potential for bad things to happen.

Your network-accessible vehicle

Some cars are already "internet ready." This doesn't mean the vehicle has wi-fi so your kids and mother-in-law can surf the web while traveling. An IoT-enabled car has an uplink to the manufacturer or dealership's systems, allowing them to alert you when you need an oil change, or to schedule routine maintenance based on your car's current conditions. Perhaps sensors will indicate the catalytic converter is going bad, or a tire is rubbing the wrong way. These are of course things you may want to have taken care of, especially if such service was part of that all-inclusive package you were upsold when you bought the car.

However, what happens if your dealership or manufacturer's website or computers get hacked? This might happen from either an outside entity or perhaps a disgruntled employee. The hacked content can include access to your personal information. In fact, it could go far beyond having simple access to your Social Security number, driver's license, and even credit card numbers... which is bad enough. What if the hacker were able to change the fuel-to-air ratio of your vehicle while you were driving? What if they could engage your anti-lock brakes while you were traveling at 70 MPH?

Whitehat hackers looking to help manufacturers better secure their data centers have already proven these are realistic possibilities. How can you protect yourself?

Being aware of the potential pitfalls of an increasingly networked world, where every product purchased can be web-enabled, is the first step to protecting ourselves, our families, and our businesses.

Making informed decisions when turning on or leaving on "phone home" capabilities of products, and keeping an inventory of which products regularly report on your personal or business habits, is the next step. Ensuring default username and passwords are disabled, to cut down on the likelihood of random strangers accessing those web-enabled devices, is the third step.

Finally, stay up to date on the latest hacks, attacks, breaches and transgressions by subscribing to a service that will alert you to problems as they are discovered and tracked.

Go to
https://keepmesafe.club/alerts
to claim your gift now.

Privacy

In Chapter 6 we addressed some of the popular door cameras like Google Nest and Ring Doorbell. While these devices have a lot of upside, there are some privacy concerns that have been raised and hyped in the media. Along with the outdoor cameras, some of the indoor cameras have problems as well. There have unfortunately been a number of documented incidents where the products performed exactly as intended... but not as *desired*.

Some people install "nanny cams" where homeowners can watch their children and babysitters during the day. Many brands are equipped with speakers and microphones so users on both sides of the connection can have conversations. These devices phone home, register, and can be accessed via a website the manufacturer created. Owners log in to check on the children.

These devices are on a potentially secure platform, but for many, the generic or default passwords are left in place. A series of articles reported on the fact that individuals were taken advantage of and spied upon. Some hackers watched or streamed video of people walking around their homes naked. In one instance, a hacker used the microphone system to broadcast into the homes and scare people.

Even more frightening, there are documented cases where young children were being interacted with by strangers in this same way. In late 2019, a Memphis family had installed such a system in their home.[7] On a day when one parent was at work and the other was outside, a stranger contacted the nine-year-old girl in the house he'd been stalking for a number of weeks, encouraging her to hurt herself. Fortunately, the young girl alerted a parent, and luckily they were able to discover what was going on.

The Internet of Things is a *George Jetson* type of life. Unfortunately, as with many tech advances, it can more closely resemble a *Minority Report* horror show.

It's not that the technology is inherently *evil*, and it's not that the interconnectivity of devices is *bad*. It would be helpful to know when a circuit is about to blow, or when a wire was about to short out to avoid a potential fire... or to prevent a more terrible outcome. It would be good to know that I have an oil leak in my car before I leave

to drive across the desert and get stranded. However, the potential for misuse and abuse is too great at this point, with too few safety features in place.

I would like to be assured that when I put my child into a car, that the vehicle is safe and will perform the way it's supposed to. I can appreciate having real-time feedback that things are working properly. However, we also need to understand what happens when we release the genie from the bottle.

---

[7] https://www.washingtonpost.com/nation/2019/12/12/she-installed-ring-camera-her-childrens-room-peace-mind-hacker-accessed-it-harassed-her-year-old-daughter/

The majority of people in the world are nice and good-hearted, fair and honest. But the majority is not everyone. There's some sliver of society that is not inherently nice and good-hearted. When asked why he robbed banks, Willy Sutton replied, "Because that's where the money is."

1950's privacy concerns vs. today

So why are people being scammed on the internet? Why is our privacy being breached? Why do people take advantage of poorly protected internet-accessible systems?

Because that's where the opportunities are.

Fear IoT?

There's no need to fear the Internet of Things but we should educate ourselves and be aware of it. Consider the difference between defending a house that has only one door and no windows to defending a mansion with hundreds of windows and tens of doors. The more potential entry points, the more difficult it will be to protect the structure.

For a networked homeowner, this is the difference between only defending the wi-fi router, versus a number of network-accessible appliances that are installed at the house—many of which have default passwords, and some number of them maintain an uplink to the manufacturer. The potential for intrusion radically increases.

Mainly because of the concerns raised around privacy, industry and governmental moves to address these concerns have begun. It is important to stay aware and up to date on where the legislation and technology trends are going to keep yourself and your family safe.

Go to
https://keepmesafe.club/alerts
to claim your gift now.

CONCLUSION

My goal for this book is not to frighten you, but rather to make you aware of the potential problems and pitfalls in our modern, networked lives. The more knowledgeable you are, the better you can protect yourself, your business, and your family.

Remember the exercise where I asked you to go Google yourself? Once you become aware of the kinds of information routinely and publicly available online about you, your business, and even your children, the more prepared you will be when someone tries to use it to bully you or someone you love into taking a harmful action. Additionally, you can work to actively mitigate negative information—like unflattering photographs—that you don't want to have released to the world. Today's online data lives forever, so be very careful what actually gets posted!

Hopefully the financial awareness you've gained here about the various scams that exist will allow you to prepare, and by extension prepare your colleagues, neighbors, and elderly relatives. Credit card and bank withdrawals resulting from hacks and scams can frequently be avoided if using multifactor authentication—a two- or three-step process that verifies each login to your accounts. My hope is now that you understand how important it is to have this in place, you will take advantage of tools from reputable sources.

In addition to the phishing and spear phishing email hacks we focused on, be aware that new scams are on the rise each week, hoping to expose your bank account, so always verify that you are replying to valid email addresses. Social engineering triggers will try to trick you to make concessions digitally and even in real life, so remain vigilant!

In May, June, and July 2021, three successive major attacks highlighted the vulnerabilities in the cybersecurity space in the United States. In May, Colonial Pipeline was hacked. While the hack that took place hit non-critical operational systems, Colonial Pipeline took their systems offline to ensure they were not further damaged or created problems within the U.S. infrastructure. The company transports oil-related products from raw oil through high-octane jet fuel from the Gulf of Mexico all the way up the East Coast to Massachusetts. When Colonial Pipeline shut down their distribution system, there were rolling fuel shortages creeping up from Florida through the southeast into the mid-Atlantic states. Photographs documented people hoarding gasoline in plastic shopping bags and five-gallon containers in the back of their station wagons. Major airlines rerouted traffic and canceled flights because jet fuel was unavailable for up to three weeks in some places, disrupting flights and a recovering economy as the COVID-19 pandemic of 2020-2021 was beginning to wane. The economic impact is still not fully known. Colonial Pipeline paid $5 million in ransomware, though about $4.5 million of it was recovered by the FBI.

About 30 days later there was an attack on JBS meat processing facilities nationwide. That attack took the processing facilities offline that supply 25% of the beef and 20% of the pork to the U.S. Keep in mind, this occurred just before the July 4th holiday weekend through the summer grilling season. JBS is said to have paid $11 million in ransomware to recover from the attack.

Time to put cybersecurity tools into motion for your family and business!

Finally, on July 2, a Friday afternoon, a major attack took out a company that most people had never heard of—Kaseya. Kaseya provides remote control and monitoring tools to Managed Service Providers, companies that manage the networks of companies, large and small. It is believe about 1500 companies were directly affected (full system and data encryption). However, tens of thousands of companies ended up taking their Kaseya systems offline for up to 21 days as the company worked to ensure vulnerabilities were not still present in their product and to assure customers not directly affected would not bring their systems back online only to then be encrypted. This affected U.S. companies, some governmental agencies, and companies worldwide. A grocery chain in Sweden had thousands of machines encrypted. The total cost of this hack is not yet known but Kaseya paid the ransom-generating company $50 million for a universal unlock key. Kaseya was preparing to go public with a large stock offering at the end of the summer 2021. They have since postponed their plans and several high-ranking officials are expected to lose their jobs.

One of your biggest potential vulnerabilities is that of not changing the default usernames and passwords on devices used in your home and business. Even if you feel your computer and network may have nothing to hide, remember that if your computer is hacked, whether business or personal, it can be utilized to further other phishing scams and hacks, imitating your email address and accessing your contacts list. Through the use of password management tools, you can create and easily retrieve stronger passwords to avoid such threats in the future, while you personally only need to remember one password to access your password management system. You can also use such a system to easily grant and withdraw password access by employees of your business. If someone quits or gets fired, you can take action within seconds.

Know that not all persons presenting themselves as repairmen or delivery people are legit. Remember the U.S. Chamber of Commerce breach through their network-enabled thermostats. With the innovations brought by the Internet of Things, all the devices connected to your network allow for the possibility of being hacked.

In this modern age of rampant ransomware attacks, having accurate and complete backups of your data can mean the difference between virtually no downtime for you and your business, versus costly ransom payments that may only leave you feeling more vulnerable to future threats.

When you consider what data to back up and how, remember RPO—recovery point objective, the time at which you wish to recover data from—and RTO—recovery time objective, the amount of time it will take to restore all your data. Even if you are routinely backing up all your content to a cloud-share service, bear in mind the differences between full and differential backups. If your last full backup was years ago, the time you saved by making routine differential backups will not be worth the time you'll lose during the restore process. Perhaps even more important is the need to assure data fidelity, verifying that the content you are restoring is accurate and valid.

In the Internet of Things, having a network-enabled toaster oven and coffee pot may make your morning flow more effortlessly, but the number of different hacking opportunities also increases exponentially. Be aware of not only privacy concerns, but also safety issues that may be introduced. It's great to warm up your vehicle with an app-click on your cell phone, but not so great to have your brakes and suspension system controlled by an outside party.

While not the end-all-be-all on the subject of hacking, cybersecurity, and privacy protection in the digital age, I do think it is a good primer on how to keep yourself and your business safe, spot potential fraud, and become more resilient.

Don't allow this increased knowledge to lead to paranoia. Instead, learn to trust but verify... as you embrace the exciting future of our increasingly interconnected digital world!